Communication for Development

Praise for this book

'Noske-Turner has assembled a formidable list of contributors who show the enormous possibilities of blending research and practice in communication for development and social change. Drawing from a range of global programmes, the articles document the dynamics of participatory experiences, the power of sophisticated evaluation methods, and the richness of practice-based thinking. The book is packed with insights and lessons that should be of interest to scholars and practitioners.'

Silvio Waisbord, Professor in the School of Media and Public Affairs,
George Washington University

Communication for Development
An evaluation framework in action

Edited by
Jessica Noske-Turner

Practical
ACTION
PUBLISHING

Practical Action Publishing Ltd
27a Albert Street, Rugby,
Warwickshire, CV21 2SG, UK
www.practicalactionpublishing.org

A catalogue record for this book is available from the British Library.
A catalogue record for this book has been requested from the Library of Congress.

ISBN 978-1-85339-997-8 Paperback
ISBN 978-1-85339-996-1 Hardback
ISBN 978-1-78044-996-8 Library PDF
ISBN 978-1-78044-997-5 Epub

Citation: Noske-Turner, J. (ed.) (2020) *Communication for Development:
An evaluation framework in action*, Practical Action Publishing, Rugby, UK
<http://dx.doi.org/10.3362/9781780449968>.

Since 1974, Practical Action Publishing has published and disseminated books
and information in support of international development work throughout
the world. Practical Action Publishing is a trading name of Practical Action
Publishing Ltd (Company Reg. No. 1159018), the wholly owned publishing
company of Practical Action. Practical Action Publishing trades only in support
of its parent charity objectives and any profits are covenanted back to Practical
Action (Charity Reg. No. 247257, Group VAT Registration No. 880 9924 76).

Cover design by RCO.design
Typeset by vPrompt eServices, India
Printed on demand

Contents

Tables, box and figures

Tables

Box

Figures

Acknowledgements

This book exists because of the belief, commitment, and contributions of many people and organizations. The book is a product of the *Evaluating Communication for Development: Supporting Adaptive and Accountable Development* research project, funded by the Australian Research Council (LP130100176) and the UNICEF C4D Section in New York. The funds from this ARC Linkage project have also enabled this book to be available open access, which is a wonderful gift to the field.

As a collaboration between RMIT University, the University of Hyderabad, and UNICEF C4D, this project benefited from the leadership of its chief and partner investigators: Jo Tacchi, Patricia Rogers, Vinod Pavarala, Linje Manyozo, and Rafael Obregón (UNICEF). Beyond their collective drive and vision for the project, and their leadership on the chapters in this book, they have been invaluable and generous mentors to me personally. Each in their different ways, they have offered challenges and new perspectives during a most formative time in my career as a postdoctoral researcher associated with the project. On behalf of the team, I would also like to extend our thanks to the two research assistants working on the project: Ho Anh Tung and Jharna Brahma.

The spark for this book, and the 22-strong authorship team it assembled, first came from Rafael Obregón, Chief of UNICEF C4D. It was his insistence that a book about the project could not be written without co authorship with colleagues from the offices in the seven countries that had been involved in the research project that set us on this course. He was right – their contributions ground the insights in a reality, and the process of co-writing itself was continually surprising and enriching. At the same time, it was no small undertaking. Throughout the editorial processes, I was acutely aware of the sacrifices being made, particularly by the practitioner authors, to make the chapters a reality. They juggle a super-human number of programmes, emails, and other demands, and writing and reviewing the chapters regularly ate into their late evenings and weekends. Particular appreciation therefore goes to the authors for their commitment and engagement. By extension, and with the chief and partner investigators, we acknowledge and thank all those who participated and contributed to the broader research activities and findings.

I finally wish to thank the team at Practical Action Publishing, who have been patient believers throughout the longer than anticipated process of bringing together the book. In particular, I thank Clare Tawney for her endurance and continued support for what is in many ways quite an unorthodox book. I am also grateful to the anonymous reviewer for insightful critiques that have pushed this book forward.

Jessica Noske-Turner
Institute for Media and Creative Industries
Loughborough University London

Foreword

A brief history of this journey

It is widely accepted that the history of Communication for Development (C4D) is inherently tied to the history of the field of development. Academics have written extensively about how communication processes and approaches have been positioned, practised, and studied over the past 60 plus years. Throughout that process they have provided a rich and diverse account of institutional practice, homegrown initiatives, critical perspectives, and innovation that paint a picture of a dynamic field that is constantly evolving and rethinking itself to remain relevant and influential in the broader development field.

This book unfolds an exciting initiative that brought together, between 2014 and 2018, three teams (the global Communication for Development Section of the United Nations Children's Fund, C4D and evaluation researchers from Royal Melbourne Institute of Technology (RMIT University), and researchers from the University of Hyderabad) with the purpose of addressing some of the most pressing questions for C4D over the past few years, considering the increased focus in the development field on evidence-based strategies and interventions and results-based management. In essence, C4D practitioners are asked to provide available evidence in order to guide strategic choices on what interventions to prioritize, and also to demonstrate the extent to which a given intervention has led to measurable changes. While we also acknowledge that a significant amount of work that takes place in the C4D field places greater emphasis on the communication process itself, the focus on measurable results is inevitable, particularly for organizations such as UNICEF.

UNICEF has a global footprint in rights-based development and humanitarian work. C4D is one of UNICEF's core implementation strategies to achieve its goals in support of children's rights worldwide. While C4D has been central to UNICEF's work for decades, in the past few years the organization has made significant investments to integrate C4D more strategically across its programmatic priorities, strengthen its C4D capacity as well as the capacity of its government and civil society counterparts, and implement evidence-based C4D strategies that take into account the questions outlined above across the spectrum of the Sustainable Development Goals (SDGs).

The roots of the initiative discussed throughout the chapters of this book go back to 2011 when UNICEF, within the context of the then C4D Roundtable of the UN, commissioned the development of the UN Inter-agency 'Resource Pack on Research, Monitoring and Evaluation in

Communication for Development'. Researchers June Lennie and Jo Tacchi led this process, with a first report titled *Researching, Monitoring and Evaluating Communication for Development: Trends, Challenges and Approaches*. In their conclusions, Lennie and Tacchi wrote:

> Participatory approaches to R, M&E have been shown, over many decades, to be very appropriate and effective for C4D. However, the political will to invest in these approaches is often weak or absent, since they tend to be perceived as too time consuming and costly. A long-term perspective is required in relation to the use of participatory methodologies, given their numerous benefits, including flexibility of the process, increased ownership of the evaluation, better utilisation of evaluation results and recommendations, and strengthened evaluation capacities. (p. 35)

Lennie and Tacchi also underscored the importance of approaching research and evaluation of C4D strategies through a holistic perspective that recognizes the complexity of development, especially when it is intended to be genuinely participatory, and the use of mixed methods that draw on the utility of quantitative and qualitative research methods while considering organizational dynamics and contexts.

Thus, when the RMIT team, led by Jo Tacchi, approached UNICEF's global C4D section to work on this initiative, it made perfect sense to embark on a collaborative journey to foster a dialogue with country-level teams, government and CSO partners, and other relevant actors on the ground to explore the application of participatory research methods in assessing the contribution of C4D strategies to address development priorities in health, water and sanitation, and child protection in combination with a reflexive process among participating teams to the role played by organizational dynamics.

While the chapters included in this book by no means exhaust the debate about how best to evaluate the contribution of C4D strategies to key development outcomes, they do provide insightful perspectives, based on relevant practice, that we hope will enrich the implementation of innovative research and monitoring and evaluation approaches. For UNICEF – and, we hope, for many other development agencies that rely heavily on the role of communication to advocate for children's rights and achieve the ambitious agenda of the SDGs – these accounts will continue to inform our strategic thinking across development practice, capacity development, and key investments to sustain the relevance of C4D strategies in the global development agenda.

I would like to acknowledge the engagement and commitment of all the partners involved in this initiative, and most particularly the UNICEF C4D teams at headquarters, regional, and country office level who made this initiative possible. I certainly hope that this constitutes an important contribution to the growth of this field, to delivering improved development outcomes, and to informing efforts towards participation-driven social change.

Rafael Obregón
Country Representative UNICEF Paraguay
Former Global Chief, Communication for Development Section, Programme
Division, UNICEF, New York

CHAPTER 1

Operationalizing a framework for C4D evaluation

Jessica Noske-Turner

Since its publication in 2013, the Evaluating Communication for Development (C4D) framework by June Lennie and Jo Tacchi has been widely welcomed as a positive and comprehensive intervention into a vexed challenge in the practice of C4D. It proposed a framework for approaching evaluation in a way that reflects the nature of C4D as a participatory, adaptive, and culturally embedded process. This chapter introduces how the framework was operationalized through a research collaboration between academics and C4D professionals. It provides an overview of the key output of the project, a co-created Evaluating C4D Resource Hub. It closes by explaining the conceptual approach to the book, which is inspired by Appreciative Inquiry, and by providing a contextual overview of the chapters.

Keywords: appreciative inquiry; communication for development; evaluation; framework; RM&E; participatory action research; UNICEF

Introduction

Perspectives on how best to monitor and evaluate communication for development (C4D) are diverse and, at times, polemic. There are those who, in seeking 'hard evidence' to promote C4D programming, have gravitated towards larger and more complicated logical frameworks or results frameworks, usually in the form of unwieldy spreadsheets with long lists of predetermined indicators for inputs, outputs, outcomes, and impacts, often depending heavily on Knowledge, Attitudes, and Practices (KAP) surveys or similar. Many are also attracted to the promises of experimental and quasi-experimental designs to deliver 'hard evidence' of impact. These are the most dominant or highly regarded approaches, and there is both internal and external pressure to use them. These are the approaches, it is often believed, that would finally prove the importance of C4D, if we could only get them right. This desire stems, in part, from a long-standing sense that for decades C4D has been marginal and misunderstood (Gumucio-Dagron and Rodríguez, 2006; Quarry and Ramírez, 2009; Gumucio-Dagron, 2008). The problem is that these approaches often lead to reducing social change to simple, linear cause-and-effect relationships, so that they fit into log frames, or can be artificially separated from other variables.

http://dx.doi.org/10.3362/9781780449968.001

Indeed, one conclusion from an attempt to undertake a randomized controlled trial of C4D was that '[l]ess complex designs ... and a tighter control over implementing agencies are likely to strengthen future impact evaluations of similar projects' (Fink et al., 2018: iv). This suggestion makes C4D the servant of its evaluation, and if followed, the advice could have the perverse effect of diminishing the potential of C4D to have any impacts in order that those impacts could be better measured.

At the other end of the spectrum, there are those who argue that C4D and the social change impacts cannot be adequately captured by such approaches. C4D, it has been argued, has more adaptive processes, which are developed in collaboration with partners and various groups, requiring flexibility to be responsive to emerging insights and changes in the local context and environment. Here, it is particularly important to revisit the definition of C4D. Fraser and Restrepo-Estrada define it as the 'use of communication processes, techniques and media to help people toward a full awareness of their situation and their options for change', emphasizing processes of consensus, conflict resolution, and planning actions for change (1998: 63). UNICEF, one of the largest agencies actively using C4D, has a definition that shares many similarities, stating a focus on developing understanding and self-awareness, identifying options, and organizing actions:

> C4D involves understanding people, their beliefs and values, the social and cultural norms that shape their lives. It involves engaging communities and listening to adults and children as they identify problems, propose solutions and act upon them. Communication for development is seen as a two-way process for sharing ideas and knowledge using a range of communication tools and approaches that empower individuals and communities to take actions to improve their lives.[1]

Lennie and Tacchi's (2013) Evaluating C4D framework is at the forefront of the latter position. Their book, *Evaluating Communication for Development: A Framework for Social Change*, was the first to comprehensively present an alternative framework for evaluation, one that was not only specific to C4D, but was informed by the principles of C4D. The framework itself comprises of seven interconnected components (participatory, holistic, complex, critical, emergent, realistic, and learning-based – these are unpacked later in this chapter). Their framework is paradigmatically distinct from the positivist-informed and management-driven results-based and experimental approaches described above. However, it is not a rejection of 'rigour' or of the value of quantitative methods. Rather, it challenges the assumptions within mainstream and dominant approaches to evaluation, about how to achieve useful, trustworthy, and credible research, monitoring, and evaluation (RM&E). The authors state that the book was intended to:

> demonstrate the value and rigour of participatory and mixed methods approaches to evaluation and the important role of evaluation in the ongoing development and improvement of C4D initiatives. We propose

that the framework can help to reinforce the case for effective two-way communication and dialogue as central and vital components of participatory forms of development and evaluation that seek positive social change. (Lennie and Tacchi, 2013: 1)

The book was positively received (see Waisbord, 2013; Unwin, 2014; Ramírez and Quarry, 2016); however, barriers to implementing the framework remained. The gap between the mainstream expectations of evaluation and the more C4D-informed approaches was now defined, but in practice little had changed. One reason was that Lennie and Tacchi's (2013) book and its framework were intentionally conceptual, and so it required further research and action to find out how the framework could be applied in practice. This was the key motivation of a collaborative research project entitled *Evaluating Communication for Development: Supporting Adaptive and Accountable Development*, which ran from 2014 to 2017. The project provided an unprecedented opportunity to apply and ground the framework in practice within UNICEF. It was driven by the goal of 'bridging the divide' between accountability-driven and learning-based evaluation approaches through operationalization with practitioners. The 'bridge' between the two should not necessarily be thought of as seeking to find a compromise between two poles. Rather, by focusing on the principles in tandem with the practical needs, the bridge is formed through practice by bringing an awareness to the choices available for evaluation, and to the implications of the choices. The chapters in this book reflect on the experiences and insights from applying the framework.

Participatory action research: bridging another divide

This book emerges from an Australian Research Council-funded research project involving RMIT, University of Hyderabad and partnering with UNICEF C4D Headquarters.[2] Through the C4D team at UNICEF's Headquarters Office, the project worked with the Eastern and Southern Africa Regional Office (Nairobi) and six country offices (Kenya, Tanzania, Malawi, Uganda, Vietnam, and India). These offices were identified as having good capacity and an interest in engaging in collaborative research around evaluation. Through those seven offices, the project also worked with UNICEF's partners in government and non-government sectors. It was therefore an opportunity to bridge another kind of divide – a divide between academia and practice.

The research project used a participatory action research (PAR) approach (Kindon et al., 2007) to engage with UNICEF and their partners in cycles of describing and reflecting on challenges and processes, creating resources and tools, using them in practice, and reviewing and reflecting on outcomes. In retrospect, it seems that the context of our use of PAR is quite unique. Typically, PAR is used with marginalized groups with an intention to create positive, empowering, and collective action types of changes. Here, PAR was being used with highly respected, knowledgeable, busy professionals.

They have high-pressure roles and significant responsibilities for large programmes, and they depended on maintaining relationships and trust among high-level government and non-government people and organizations for the functioning of their programmes. In short, they came to the partnership with particular ideas and expectations about how the project could benefit their work, and they had much more at stake than the academics if our 'trials' and 'experiments' of new approaches did not go to plan.

This relationship and dynamics between the academic and practitioner members of the partnership took some adjustment. At times, collaborators on the UNICEF side seemed to want to relate to the academics either as experts (who direct UNICEF on what it should do) or as consultants (who UNICEF directs on what they should do). The pendulum would often swing between these positions, rarely resting in the middle. On the other side, the academics also had a learning curve. Although we said that we did not want to be 'experts', sometimes we probably acted like them. At times, we assumed that our approach and perspectives were the answer and settled into critiquing at an easy, detached distance. In one particular workshop the true vulnerability of both positions was unmasked. The workshop involved government partners in Vietnam (for more, see Tran et al., 2020). Progress had stalled, the resources were not working, and with the discomfort rising, the illusion that the academic in the room was an 'expert' crumbled. It was a revelatory moment about the work-in-progress nature of the ideas, the high stakes at play, but also the reason why the collaboration between academics, with their theories and concepts, and practitioners, with their years of accumulated 'practical wisdom' (Quarry and Ramírez, 2018), was so valuable.

This is therefore quite an unorthodox use of PAR, collaborating with practitioners who are high-powered and in many respects quite empowered professionals in the context of the development sector, and who are simultaneously constantly struggling with heavy workloads, limited budgets, and negotiations over decision making, and managing competing pressures from upper levels of management, which combine to restrict their individual power to challenge systematic demands on C4D and evaluation. The purpose of PAR in this unusual context was therefore to build on existing capacity, empowering practitioners to use their knowledge, ideas, and learning about C4D evaluation effectively within all the well-known constraints, while also encouraging critical attention to the systems and practices that perpetuate problems.

Overview of the Evaluating C4D Resource Hub

As anyone who has ever done a search for resources for evaluation will have quickly learned, there is no shortage of toolkits and guides available. One inherent problem with toolkits, however, is that they tend to be either too broad and vague, or too prescriptive and specific. Tools designed around steps are also problematic, assuming that everyone is starting from the beginning, when, in practice, due to staff turnover and other issues, practitioners rarely have the luxury of starting with a clean slate and seeing a project from conception to completion. Our team came to know these issues intimately, because the early iterations of what became the Evaluating C4D Resource Hub suffered from all of these problems.

Several different iterations were created and trialled, all intending to support the generation of better insight, evidence, and evaluation of C4D. The final Evaluating C4D Resource Hub is in a sense an anti-toolkit, in keeping with Lennie and Tacchi's pledge 'not to create another toolkit' (2011: 3). It is instead proposed as a curated hub of existing resources, with a meaningful structure that helps practitioners reflect on options and implications of different approaches and ultimately choose methods and tools that are consistent with the values and needs of C4D.

The Evaluating C4D Resource Hub, the key output emerging from the participatory action research, will now be introduced in detail, since the experiences shared in the remaining chapters in this book in some way contributed to informing it, or are examples of the kinds of research and evaluation initiatives it hopes to support and inspire.

The Evaluating C4D Resource Hub is structured around two combined frameworks:

- the Evaluating C4D framework (Lennie and Tacchi, 2013), which is a *conceptual* framework describing an *approach* to evaluation based on the values and principles that are consistent with a view of C4D as a participatory, social, and communicative process of engagement;
- the Rainbow framework (BetterEvaluation.org), which is a *structure* that organizes the practical tasks associated with RM&E into seven categories or 'clusters', and provides options.

The Evaluating C4D framework includes seven components (see Box 1.1 and Figure 1.1), referred to on the Resource Hub as 'principles'. These include that C4D RM&E should be: participatory, in keeping with C4D's emphasis on inclusion and dialogue; holistic, with an awareness of local contexts, systems, and inter-relations; complex, problematizing simplistic cause-and-effect models in favour of emergence, and anticipating the need to remain flexible and adaptable; critical and conscious of issues of power and difference; realistic, taking a pragmatic approach, grounded and engaged with participants; and learning-based, focused on capacity development and active learning. Throughout this project the concepts associated with Lennie and Tacchi's *emergent* component were integrated into *complex*, *learning-based* and *holistic*; and *accountable* was added as the seventh principle.

The seven principles of the Evaluating C4D Resource Hub framework

A detailed explanation of each of the seven, interconnected principles as they were adapted for the online Evaluating C4D Resource Hub is shown in Box 1.1.

Box 1.1 Overview of the seven principles for the Evaluating C4D framework

Participatory

Participation is a central principle for C4D, and therefore should be incorporated in the RM&E of C4D. Participatory RM&E is undertaken in partnership with children and adolescents, community members, and other stakeholders, using processes that are culturally and socially appropriate, creative, and based on mutual trust, openness, and dialogue.

Holistic

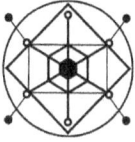

Taking a holistic approach means considering the systems, structures, and contexts within which people operate. This means seeking to understand the broader contexts and interconnections between organizations, groups, and individuals involved in a C4D initiative (directly or indirectly). This might include the different 'communicative ecologies' (or communication contexts) that people experience.

Complex

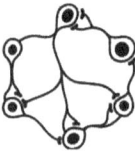

The principle of complexity draws our attention to the multiple and changing 'interconnections' and 'inter-relationships' in C4D initiatives. It highlights complicated aspects: where there are multiple organizations working in similar ways, multiple components or parts of the initiative, or where we know that C4D interventions will work differently in different contexts. It also highlights complex aspects: where change is not predictable but comes about through 'adaptive' responses to changing circumstances.

Critical

Including different perspectives highlights the importance of paying critical attention to power. Our approach to RM&E needs to actively address issues of equity and diversity by paying attention to gender, class, and other relevant differences. Design and implementation of RM&E can build on the strengths and limitations of different evaluation approaches and methods, to find the right approaches for your evaluation questions and include all relevant voices and perspectives.

Accountable

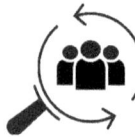

Accountability means demonstrating results to communities, partners, funders, and policymakers. RM&E that is rigorous, transparent, and relevant will produce evidence for accountability. In C4D our primary responsibility is to be listening to, learning from, and reporting to community groups and partners. Achieving account-ability depends on having clear and shared expectations about what is to be evaluated, what the evaluation questions are, and how you will go about answering them. Understanding who you are accountable to also requires clarity.

Realistic

To be most effective, RM&E approaches and methods need to be grounded in local realities. This requires openness, freedom, flexibility, and realism in planning and implementing RM&E and in the selection of approaches, methodologies, and methods. This approach aims to increase the usefulness of evaluation results, which should focus on intended, unintended, expected, unexpected, negative, and positive change. Long-term engagement with organizations and communities ensures effectiveness and sustainability, and a long-term perspective on both evaluation and social change.

| **Learning-based**  | In a learning-based approach, RM&E is integrated into the whole programme cycle and involves all staff and stakeholders. This principle draws on some of the core principles of action learning and PAR, including iterative reflection on implementation for continual improvement. Involving a broad group of stakeholders in RM&E requires attention to capacity development and learning processes and events. |

Source: Lennie and Tacchi (2013), as adapted for the Evaluating C4D Resource Hub.

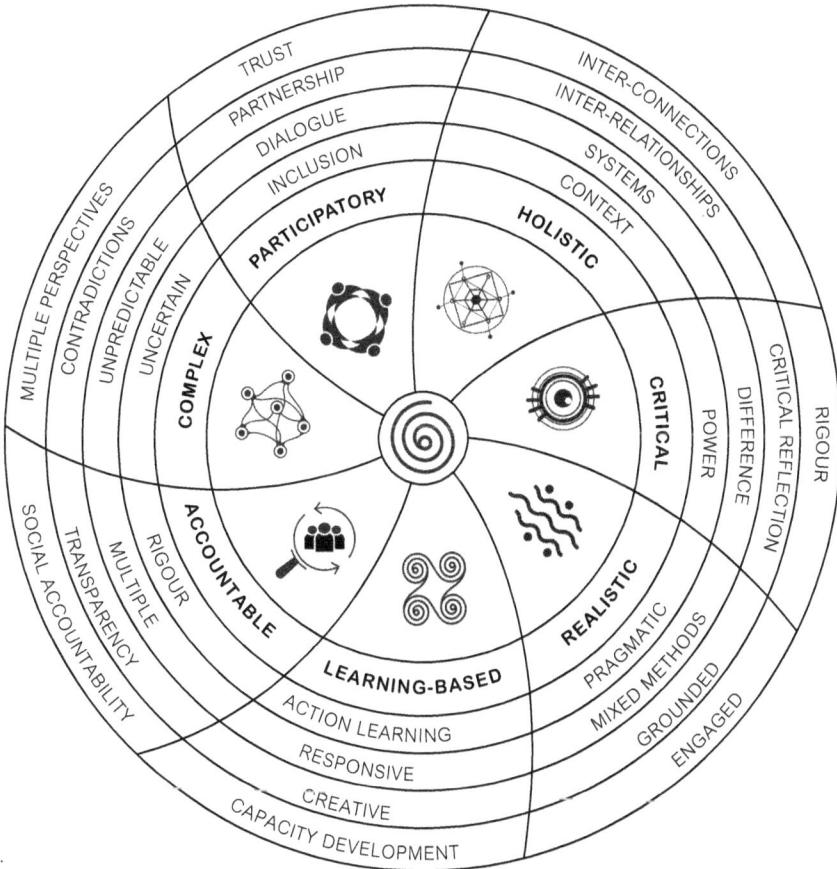

Figure 1.1 Evaluating C4D Resource Hub framework
Source: Adapted from Lennie and Tacchi (2013) to include 'accountable'

A note on being 'accountable'

The purpose of incorporating accountability as one of the seven principles was to reinterpret and challenge the dominant meaning of accountability from a C4D perspective. 'Accountability' is referenced in the subtitle of the research project 'supporting adaptive and accountable development'. Furthermore, occasionally the need to be 'accountable' for doing good with the funds for development was mentioned in some workshops and interviews, although often this was under-interrogated and brushed off as common sense. Integrating accountability as one of the principles was a way to explicitly address the meaning of accountability in the context of C4D and evaluation and in dialogue with the other principles. In this context, the principle aligns with Wilkin's (2018) exploration of accountability, evaluation, and justice, where she argues that there should be a greater focus on actually using research and evaluation to improve development initiatives as a form of accountability, conceptualizing this as a form of social justice to the global community, including citizens in both donor countries and recipient countries. By making explicit references to accountability communities and partners, alongside the usual drivers of accountability upwards to funders and policymakers, this intervention contributes to making a statement on what it means to bridge 'accountability' and 'learning-based' approaches in the context of C4D principles and approaches. It draws closer to Manyozo's more radical definition of C4D as the 'employment of media and communication to interrupt and transform the political economy of development in ways that enable individuals, communities and societies to determine their own history' (Manyozo, 2017: 81). Defining 'accountability' in these terms demands a participatory and co-created evaluation in order to open up the learning process for partners and organizations in transparent and committed ways.

The Rainbow framework

Turning to the second framework, the Rainbow framework (Figure 1.2) is a way of structuring evaluation practice. It names more than 30 research, monitoring, and evaluation 'tasks' (such as 'develop a theory of change'; 'develop reporting media') and organizes these into seven categories referred to as 'clusters'. In fact, BetterEvaluation.org itself can be thought of as a 'hub of resources'. Crucially, these clusters are not sequential, and users are encouraged to dip in and out of tasks depending on the needs of the project as it progresses. It has been developed to support evaluation practitioners across a range of evaluation domains (i.e. government, non-profit, international development, private sector, etc.), to wide acclaim on the part of practitioners in the field.

Bringing these two frameworks together means that the C4D-informed principles can be applied like a filter when viewing the tasks within the Rainbow framework, in order to weigh up the value and benefit of using various methods, options, tools, and strategies. Case studies showing these principles

The Better Evaluation Rainbow Framework can be used to plan an evaluation or to locate information about particular types of options.

Manage

Define

Frame

Describe

Understand causes

Synthesize

Report & support use

Tasks

1. Sample
2. Use measures, indicators or metrics
3. Collect/retrieve data
4. Manage data
5. Combine qualitative and quantitative data
6. Analyse data
7. Visualize data

Options

Options include:

- After action review
- Deliberative opinion polls
- Delphi study
- Interviews
- Logs and diaries
- Participant observation
- Photovoice

and many more...

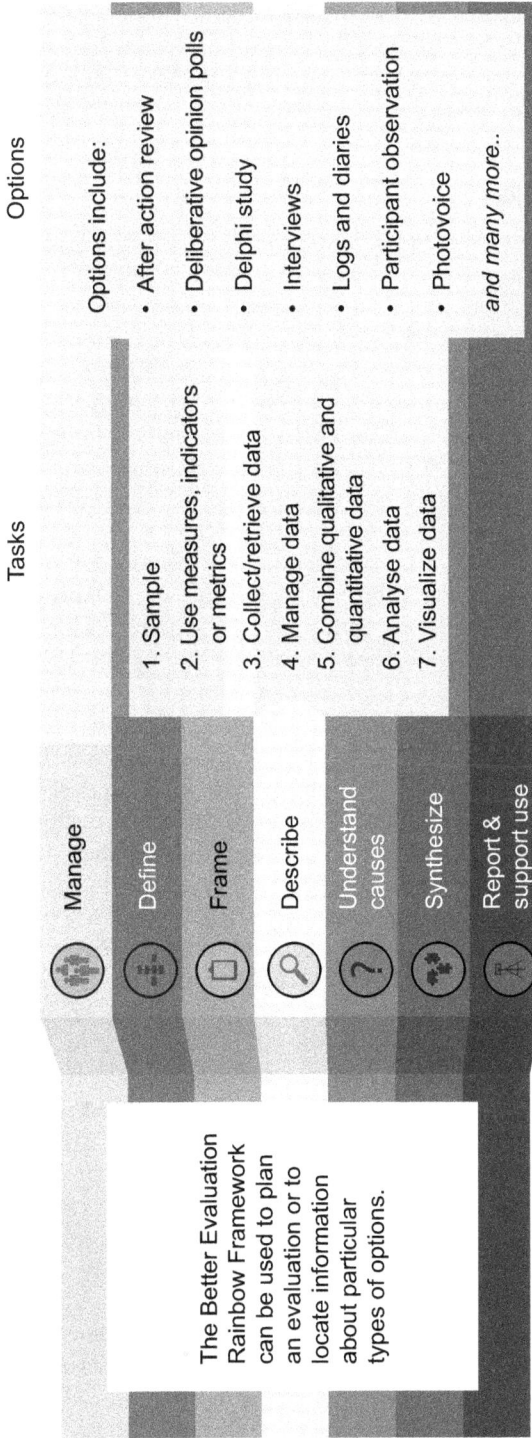

Figure 1.2 The seven 'clusters' of the Better Evaluation Rainbow framework, highlighting the 'tasks' and some of the 'options' found under 'Describe'
Source: <https://www.betterevaluation.org/en/rainbow_framework> [accessed 22 November 2019]

in action and additional resources used by practitioners were incorporated in the Resource Hub, including from practitioners outside UNICEF through a crowd-sourcing effort in partnership with the C4D Network, and work to incorporate more resources and examples is a continuing project.

Overview of the book

This book presents five cases that reflect on the experiences of using practices consistent with the Evaluating C4D framework. Case studies are important to help move from a set of ideal principles to an understanding of how the framework may be operationalized within the actual realities of development institutions, organizations, and communities. The authors of each chapter focus on a few key principles from the framework and contextualize how they interpreted those principles in relation to various methods, models, and projects. As well as showing the usefulness and opportunities, they illustrate the challenges of balancing the various principles as well as real-world practical needs.

This book is infused with the very same commitment to participatory action research taken in relation to the project as a whole. Academic members of the research team partnered with practitioner-collaborators, pushing and challenging each other. The writing process was an opportunity for the practitioners involved to continue and deepen reflexivity, to create a space for introspective interrogation of the issues at their roots, and of what has been learned in the process. Equally, the academics are pushed out of their comfort zones. Critique is easy from the comfort of the metaphorical 'ivory towers', but through the act of collaborative writing there is a responsibility to be constructive in an attempt to create change. As both the editor and as an author, I observed and experienced the slow process of co-writing, watching the various chapters take shape over a series of long-distance phone or Skype calls, and through many drafts sent back and forth. In pursuit of a coherent, shared narrative, authors asked each other probing questions: *What do you mean by this? Can you explain this in a different way? Are you sure about this? Are there any other reasons why that might have happened?* Both the text that was added and the text that was deleted revealed much rich detail about the different perspectives on problems and priorities, and the plural interpretations of events and discussions. Working through the misunderstandings was crucial to emerging with an enriched and shared representation of the experience, and a deeper understanding between academics and practitioners. Co-writing itself has been among the most useful processes in the research collaboration, a method as useful as interviews and workshops for generating insights and understanding.

The approach and construction of the book is inspired by Appreciative Inquiry (taking some creative liberties) to reflect on the opportunities associated with bringing a social change-oriented framework to the tasks of RM&E of C4D. The chapters are a set of positive 'discoveries', to use the

Appreciative Inquiry term (Cooperrider et al., 2005), where, whether directly facilitated by the project or emerging independently based on a confluence of factors, practices exhibiting a communication and social change approach to evaluation have been identified. We do not claim that the cases are representative; indeed, they are worthy of our attention because they defy dominant organizational expectations and practices.

While the cases are presented here to be 'appreciated', the authors were challenged to also subject their experience to inquiry. What factors enabled the practitioners involved to overcome the common challenges in their case? How were challenges navigated and what compromises were found? What forms of resistance needed to be overcome to achieve this outcome, and how was this achieved? What would need to be considered if attempting to replicate this experience elsewhere? Grappling with these kinds of questions is crucial to learning and building on these cases.

The book opens with Percy-Smith, Bakta, Noske-Turner, Mtenga, and Portela Souza's detailed study of the use of community-based research using participatory action research to examine and develop responses to violence against children in Tanzania (Percy-Smith et al., 2020). The initiative pre-dates and was undertaken independently of the Evaluating C4D project but was shared during the early 'scoping phase' as an inspiring recent experience of research or evaluation. The initiative was motivated by C4D and Child Protection teams in UNICEF's Tanzania Country Office's recognition that the standard KAP surveys would most likely not yield useful or credible insights on this very sensitive topic. They engaged a British researcher from the University of Huddersfield, who in turn brought in researchers from the University of Tanzania, to engage communities and partners in transformative processes of dialogue and analysis, towards the construction of proposed actions for the government and UNICEF Tanzania. It illustrates many of the principles from the Evaluating C4D framework, most obviously its use of *participatory* approaches, but also for generating *holistic*, rich, and culturally embedded understandings; and its recognition of the *complexity* of the issue and context, requiring flexibility and space for emergence. The example also textures the principle of being *critical*; in this case, women challenged the decision to have gender-segregated focus groups since they felt it reinforced stereotypes and limited the necessary dialogue between the two groups. Finally, although it is not the authors' primary focus, the case was an experiment in constructing a mentoring arrangement through a consultancy partnership between Northern researchers and local Tanzanian university researchers, modelling one approach to capacity development and a *learning-based* approach.

The next case (Tran et al., 2020) continues the theme of reflecting on participatory approaches, this time undertaking a critical reflection on the efforts to use participatory approaches in Vietnam. The UNICEF Vietnam Country Office was one of the most proactive in joining and participating in the collaborative research project, and the initial workshops developed much positivity and motivation to increase the level of participation in the RM&E of C4D across various programmes. In Chapter 3, Tran, Noske-Turner, and Ho give an account of their at times quite confounding and confronting experience of trialling the work-in-progress resources within the hierarchical context of government programming. Two initiatives are discussed in detail: collaborating with a consultant to undertake an assessment, with some mixed experiences of experimenting with new approaches; and a workshop with national-level government officials attempting to co-design a monitoring and evaluation plan. In the critique of universalist packaging of 'participation', the case indirectly reinforces the importance of the *critical* principle from the framework, which requires cultural knowledge in developing appropriate strategies and methods.

Tacchi, Chandola, Pavarala and Elessawi also continue the theme of participatory approaches in Chapter 4 (Tacchi et al., 2020). Their chapter describes their experience of undertaking ethnographic 'retrospective analysis', beginning with a participatory research design process, as a way of experimenting directly with implementation of such approaches and demonstrating their usefulness. The research was instigated due to a need to understand how one district in West Bengal, India had managed to buck the trend and achieve Open Defecation Free (ODF) status, and a desire to know whether the process and outcomes were sustainable and replicable. Similar to the violence against children case outlined by Percy-Smith et al., open defecation is exceptionally sensitive, bound up with a range of cultural meanings and practices. These practices, they found, are significantly entwined with caste and class differences. The authors found that, by combining an ethnographic approach with participatory design processes, they were able to generate deeper and more nuanced understandings that were sensitive to and recognized the complexities of gendered and caste-dependent experiences.

The case by Elliott, Samati, Noske-Turner, and Rogers in Chapter 5 (Elliott et al., 2020) explores what it looks like to take 'complexity' seriously in research and evaluation from the perspective of a community-based organization. The Creative Centre for Community Mobilization (CRECCOM), directed by one of the authors (Samati), is a Malawian NGO that has participation, communication, and community engagement at its core. It has partnered with UNICEF C4D on a number of projects, and it participated in the C4D Learning Labs discussed in the following chapter. In this chapter, the authors reflect on a project with other (non-traditional) donors, where intensely flexible and adaptive implementation processes were enabled through a combination of CRECCOM's own concept of 'tepetepe' (meaning 'flexible' in the local language) and 'design learning', a method introduced by one of the partners. This level of adaptiveness, allowing the project design to evolve through continuous dialogue with stakeholders and community members, is in stark contrast to the usual demand for predetermined inputs, outputs, project milestones, and indicators. It also exemplifies why Fink et al.'s (2018) suggestion that there needs to be 'tighter control over implementing agencies' to suit the needs of experimental evaluation designs runs counter to the nature of highly effective C4D. The case provides a model for approaching intractable challenges in a 'complexity-congruent' way, and raises a challenge to donors and partners about how they can foster and support these types of approaches.

The final case (Chapter 6) stays in Malawi and shares reflections on long-term capacity-building efforts among partners on various aspects of C4D, including on RM&E, which are called C4D Learning Labs. Manyozo, Aliyev, Nkhonjera, Mauluka, and Khangamwa (2020) introduce critical perspectives on capacity building, which reveal some of the different perspectives and interests in capacity building, contrasting approaches where the primary interest is knowledge transfer, and a more generative and bottom-up view of capacity building, where existing capacities are valued, shared, and connected to enhance collective capacity. One of the C4D Learning Lab events was focused on the Evaluating C4D principles and Resource Hub when it was almost finalized. There are parallels between the tensions that Manyozo et al. are drawing out and that experience, where a mix of different interests were at play, but where there was also a commitment to fostering, connecting, and empowering the partners to examine the systems they navigate in order to conduct their work, and how that affects their opportunities and 'capacities' to implement according to the principles of the Evaluating C4D framework.

Appreciating positive cases is motivating and energizing, but what is required to make these types of cases less exceptional and more reflective of normal, everyday practices? In the concluding chapter (Noske-Turner et al., 2020), Noske-Turner, Tacchi, Obregón, Chitnis, and Lapsansky take up and explore this challenging question. This chapter draws on the 'discoveries' shared in each of the chapters, analysing the commonalities and insights they offer for informing a set of actions, with the ultimate ambition to achieve sector-wide changes in C4D evaluation.

Notes

1. <https://www.unicef.org/cbsc/> [accessed 23 April 2019].
2. ARC Linkage Project LP130100176: *Evaluating Communication for Development: Supporting Adaptive and Accountable Development*. Led by Jo Tacchi, Patricia Rogers, Vinod Pavarala, and Rafael Obregón, with Jessica Noske-Turner (postdoctoral researcher, RMIT University), Ho Anh Tung (research assistant, RMIT Vietnam), and Jharna Brahma (research assistant, University of Hyderabad).

References

Cooperrider, D., Whitney, D. and Stavros, J. (2005) *Appreciative Inquiry Handbook: The First in a Series of AI Workbooks for Leaders of Change*, Crown Custom Publishing, Brunswick OH.

Elliott, J., Samati, M.E., Noske-Turner, J. and Rogers, P. (2020) 'Using "tepetepe" for understanding the complexity of people's lives in Malawi', in J. Noske-Turner (ed.), *Communication for Development: An Evaluation Framework in Action*, Practical Action Publishing, Rugby.

Fink, G., Karlan, D., Udry, C., Osei, R., Bonargent, A. and Torres, N. (2018) *Communication for Development to Improve Health Behaviours in Ghana: 3ie Grantee Final Report*, International Initiative for Impact Evaluation (3ie), New Delhi. Available from: <https://www.3ieimpact.org/sites/default/files/2019-01/gfr-OW4.1122-health-behaviour-ghana.pdf> [accessed 22 November 2019].

Fraser, C. and Restrepo-Estrada, S. (1998) *Communicating for Development: Human Change for Survival*, I.B. Tauris, London and New York.

Gumucio-Dagron, A. (2008) 'Vertical minds versus horizontal cultures: an overview of participatory process and experiences', in J. Servaes (ed.), *Communication for Development and Social Change*, pp. 68–82, Sage, London.

Gumucio-Dagron, A. and Rodríguez, C. (2006) 'Time to call things by their name', *Media Development* 53 (3): 9–16.

Kindon, S., Pain, R. and Kesby, M. (2007) 'Participatory action research: origins, approaches and methods', in S. Kindon, R. Pain and M. Kesby (eds), *Participatory Action Research Approaches and Methods*, Routledge, Abingdon and New York.

Lennie, J. and Tacchi, J. (2011) *Outline of a Guide to Designing the Research, Monitoring and Evaluation Process for Communication for Development in the UN*, UN Interagency Group on Communication for Development, New York. Available from: <https://www.unicef.org/cbsc/files/C4D_RME-Outline_of_Guide_to_Designing_RME_for_C4D_in_the_UN_Final-2011.pdf> [accessed 22 November 2019].

Lennie, J. and Tacchi, J. (2013) *Evaluating Communication for Development: A Framework for Social Change*, Earthscan/Routledge, New York.

Manyozo, L. (2017) *Communicating Development with Communities*, Routledge, Abingdon.

Manyozo, L., Aliyev, E., Nkhonjera, P., Mauluka, C. and Khangamwa, C. (2020) 'Towards horizontal capacity building: UNICEF Malawi's C4D Learning Labs', in J. Noske-Turner (ed.), *Communication for Development: An Evaluation Framework in Action*, Practical Action Publishing, Rugby.

Noske-Tuner, J., Tacchi, J., Obregón, R., Chitnis, K. and Lapsansky, C. (2020) 'The challenges ahead: cultivating the conditions for small revolutions in C4D evaluation', in J. Noske-Turner (ed.), *Communication for Development: An Evaluation Framework in Action*, Practical Action Publishing, Rugby.

Percy-Smith, B., Bakta, S., Noske-Turner, J., Mtenga, G. and Portela Souza, P. (2020) 'Using community-based action research as a participatory alternative in responding to violence in Tanzania', in J. Noske-Turner (ed.), *Communication for Development: An Evaluation Framework in Action*, Practical Action Publishing, Rugby.

Quarry, W. and Ramírez, R. (2009) *Communication for Another Development: Listening before Telling*, Zed Books, London.

Ramírez, R. and Quarry, W. (2016) '*Evaluating Communication for Development: A Framework for Social Change*, by June Lennie and Jo Tacchi (2013, Earthscan)', *Journal of MultiDisciplinary Evaluation* 12 (26): 25–6. Available from: <http://journals.sfu.ca/jmde/index.php/jmde_1/article/view/437> [accessed 22 November 2019].

Ramírez, R. and Quarry, W. (2018) 'Communication and evaluation: can a decision-making hybrid reframe an age-old dichotomy?', in F. Enghel and J. Noske-Turner (eds), *Communication in International Development*, pp. 135–52, Routledge, Abingdon.

Tacchi, J., Chandola, T., Pavarala, V. and Elessawi, R. (2020) 'Exploring sanitation: participatory research design and ethnography in West Bengal', in J. Noske-Turner (ed.), *Communication for Development: An Evaluation Framework in Action*, Practical Action Publishing, Rugby.

Tran, P.-A., Noske-Turner, J. and Ho, A.T. (2020) 'Finding and creating opportunities for participatory approaches to RM&E in Vietnam', in J. Noske-Turner (ed.), *Communication for Development: An Evaluation Framework in Action*, Practical Action Publishing, Rugby.

Unwin, T.S. (2014) 'Evaluating communication for development', *Information Technologies and International Development* 10 (2): 63–5. Available from: <https://itidjournal.org/index.php/itid/article/viewFile/1217/483> [accessed 22 November 2019].

Waisbord, S. (2013) '*Evaluating Communication for Development: A Framework for Social Change*, by Lennie, J. and Tacchi, J.', *Communication Review* 16 (3): 178–80 <https://doi.org/10.1080/10714421.2013.807121>.

Wilkins, K.G. (2018) 'Communication about development and the challenge of doing well: donor branding in the West Bank', in F. Enghel and J. Noske-Turner (eds), *Communication in International Development*, pp. 92–112, Routledge, Abingdon.

Author biography

Jessica Noske-Turner is a lecturer in Media and Creative Industries, Loughborough University London. From 2014 to 2017 she was a postdoctoral fellow at RMIT University, contributing to the *Evaluating C4D: Supporting Adaptive and Accountable Development* research project.

CHAPTER 2

Using community-based action research as a participatory alternative in responding to violence in Tanzania

*Barry Percy-Smith, Seraphina Bakta,
Jessica Noske-Turner, Georgina Mtenga
and Patricia Portela Souza*

*Surveys to measure Knowledge, Attitudes, and Practices (KAP) are a dominant
method in the Social and Behaviour Change field. However, KAP surveys are limited
in their utility for engaging community stakeholders in developing, implementing,
and evaluating change processes. This chapter critiques KAP surveys, and makes
the case for a more engaged, learning-based participatory alternative in the form
of community-based action research. The chapter presents a case study of how
participatory action research has been used to involve stakeholders in engaging with,
and responding to, violence against children in Tanzania. This case exemplifies the
central importance of engaging community members in dialogue and inquiry to voice
the 'unspoken' in response to socio-culturally sensitive issues, to develop ownership
and solidarity in responding to community problems, and as a basis for community-
relevant actions for social change.*

Keywords: children; community-based research; Knowledge, Attitudes,
and Practices; participatory action research; Tanzania; violence

Introduction

Interpersonal violence is a major global public health issue with significant
impacts on the well-being and development of women and children as
citizens, on social well-being and equality in communities, and with implications for social and economic development in countries in the Global South.
There is now substantial research literature on the causes and consequences of
interpersonal violence (see, for example, Jones, 2013; Crosson-Tower, 2008),
and combatting violence against children (VAC) with gender-based violence
high on policy and programming agendas (UN, 2006). VAC includes specific
acts of violence and maltreatment such as physical, sexual, and psycho-
logical violence and neglect, with many children living in a state of fear,

http://dx.doi.org/10.3362/9781780449968.002

anxiety, existential insecurity, injustice and in a context of contradictory adult behaviour (Percy-Smith et al., 2017). Interpersonal violence affects individual children directly through individual acts of violence and abuse, while structural violence affects the social context and status of childhood.

In response to global issues such as violence against children, Knowledge, Attitudes, and Practices (KAP) surveys have tended to constitute the gold standard in collecting data to inform programming decisions. Yet there is increasing recognition of the limitations of KAP surveys in engaging communities in response to complex socio-cultural issues and in informing change processes (e.g. Lennie & Tacchi 2013; Launiala 2009). There has been an increasing plethora of Communication for Social Change frameworks and approaches, such as the Evaluating Communication for Development (C4D) framework (Lennie and Tacchi, 2013) and other forms of transformative and participatory approaches to development (Hickey and Mohan, 2004; Burns and Worsley, 2015), that highlight the value of broader sets of principles in research for change initiatives. Within the context of these developments, this chapter discusses the rationale and experience of using one such alternative participatory approach to engage local stakeholders in response to VAC in Tanzania. This initiative, the outcome of which is the *Report from the Study of Socio-cultural Drivers of Violence and Positive Change in Tanzania* (Percy-Smith et al., 2017), was undertaken prior to and independently of the Evaluating C4D research collaboration between researchers and UNICEF C4D (see Noske-Turner, 2020). It was identified in the early stages of the research collaborations as exemplifying the principles underpinning the Evaluating C4D framework (Lennie and Tacchi, 2013). In particular, the case illustrates the value of a participatory and learning-based approach to C4D evaluation, highlighting the importance of a flexible, emergent approach, and the need for critical inquiry as a central tenet to engage with underlying structural and gender inequalities.

Context

A survey of VAC in Tanzania in 2011 identified that one in three girls and one in six boys experience sexual abuse before they are 18 years old; 75 per cent of girls and boys experience physical violence from adults, 60 per cent at the hands of relatives, and one out of two at the hands of teachers; 83 per cent of those experiencing sexual violence also experience physical violence and 25 per cent experience emotional violence (UNICEF et al., 2011). The research revealed that many children live in a state of fear, anxiety, and existential insecurity and forgo basic human development rights such as health and education. Underlying these trends are socio-cultural practices concerning the way in which children and women are treated, gender roles, parenting practices underpinned by long-established socio-cultural norms, and patriarchal values that exert a powerful controlling influence on behaviours and resistance to the questioning of social norms, even if they are detrimental to children's well-being (Percy-Smith et al., 2017). And there are paradoxes at play. For example, many people talk about their visions of what having a good childhood involves yet continue perpetrating practices that harm children. There is widespread fear of speaking out against the status quo, against the powerful community influences that silence; and this is exacerbated by other socio-cultural traditions such as '*Muhali*', a Kiswahili term indicating tacit understanding that compels people to refrain from causing community dissonance. Hence, in the event of a young girl being raped by a member of the community, the father of the girl may seek reconciliation with the perpetrator at the expense of justice for the child.

The voice of the child in Tanzania, as in many countries in the Global South, is not considered in the socio-development discourse. In spite of widespread knowledge that rape is a crime, and despite public attitudes that condemn rape in Tanzania, rape continues. Perpetuation of the status quo through social norms that place community cohesion above deliberation to address community problems prevents behaviour change. This is mirrored by a police and judicial system that falls short of effectiveness, with many perpetrators failing to be brought to justice. The net result is that VAC continues with limited opportunities for communities to talk about or address these problems.

The role of Knowledge, Attitudes, and Practices surveys

KAP surveys are a common approach to C4D, monitoring and evaluation and research studies to inform strategy and programming. KAP surveys seek to collect information from a target population on what is known on a particular topic, opinions and beliefs about that topic, and what people actually do – their behaviours and practices.

The surveys emerged in the 1950s in the context of family planning (Cleland, 1973; Launiala, 2009) and are now used across many sectors, such as HIV/AIDS (Schopper et al., 1993) and malaria (Launiala, 2009). Conceptually, the KAP model is developed from a 'diffusion' theory of communication for behaviour change based on the idea that the provision of (appropriate) information leads to Knowledge, which in turn leads to changes in Attitudes, which then leads to changed Practices or behaviours (Morris, 2003). KAP studies are therefore most common in 'media/communication for development' approaches (Manyozo, 2012; Scott, 2014), where behaviour and social changes are the ultimate objective of communication campaigns or programmes, such as edutainment, interpersonal communication activities, or social marketing. The intention of KAP surveys is to capture social attitudes and behaviours to better inform programmes tailored to promoting behaviour change, for example with respect to gender norms or child labour (Portela de Souza, 2010). KAP surveys have almost automatic credibility in the reporting systems of development organizations such as UNICEF. The KAP typology is easily translated into the quantitative, 'SMART' (specific, measurable, achievable, relevant, and timebound) indicators required by results frameworks. Many of the available national statistics reference knowledge, attitudes, and practices, which in turn reinforces the use of KAP-based indicators.

In spite of the widespread use of KAP surveys, there has been an increasing number of questions asked concerning their efficacy in providing the strategies for change that are needed in many development contexts. KAP surveys are based on two assumptions that are taken for granted: first, that the 'knowledge provider' (the programming institution) knows what knowledge is needed (Launiala, 2009; Sparks, 2007); and second, that recipients are open, ready, and able to accept and use that knowledge to change behaviour (Sparks, 2007; Hornik, 2002). As a result of its origins in diffusion theory, the KAP model thus tends to imply one-way communication approaches from the sender to the receiver, involving a fairly linear theory of behaviour change, with little acknowledgement of the wider factors at play in local contexts, such as the complexity of socio-cultural dynamics (Percy-Smith et al., 2017) and the availability of resources to implement change. A further limitation is that KAP surveys show changes only at an individual level and ignore other levels of socio-ecological contexts (Bronfenbrenner, 1979) that are required for social change at the level of communities, services, the macro-economy, policy, and the environment. While KAP surveys serve the planning and reporting requirements of more top-down behaviour change communication programmes quite well, they are less useful when used as a mechanism for programming and capacity building, including ownership by and engagement of local stakeholders as actors of change where outcomes are relevant and meaningful for those concerned.

In response to some of the limitations and challenges outlined above, more recent developments have sought to rethink KAPs and challenge their dominance and influence within the institution (see, for example, Portela de Souza, 2010). For example, work in Bangladesh has extended the traditional KAP focus to also include social 'expectations' ('KAPE'). 'Expectations' here is a reference to theories of social norms, where people's actions can be shaped by cultural rules or expectations of 'normal', 'appropriate' behaviour. In such situations, the individual acts according to a belief that a sufficiently large part of the relevant population expects him or her to conform to a certain behaviour when faced with the same situation (Bicchieri and Mercier, 2014). While not resolving all the challenges outlined above, KAPE does allow for exploration of the extent to which behaviour (or practices) may be shaped not only by knowledge but perhaps also (or instead) by social norms. In the same way, attention is directed both at individual-level knowledge and community-level expectations that drive social norms, although structural, service access, political, and equity factors are not necessarily addressed.

KAP surveys and the Evaluating C4D framework

One way to understand some of the problems with KAP surveys as an approach is to use the Evaluating C4D framework. First, KAP surveys are not particularly *holistic*. They do not pay attention to the whole context in which knowledge, opinions, beliefs, and practices occur. 'Knowledge' refers mainly to the acquisition of modern biomedical and pragmatic information (Pelto and Pelto, 1997), with little engagement with how this interacts with other types of knowledge, such as indigenous knowledge and cultural practices (Launiala, 2009), or with relational knowledge generated in communicative action with others (Kemmis, 2001). Building on this, traditional KAP surveys leave little scope for *participation*; instead, they are usually standardized, top-down, and extractive, serving the agenda of development planners and organizations rather than being an opportunity for engagement with communities about their own contexts and opportunities for change. While this makes them useful for upward accountability, it means that they are rarely used to ensure *accountability* to local communities. KAP surveys are geared towards reporting against results frameworks, rather than being used as a mechanism for *learning* and adapting programmes. KAP surveys have pre-set, rather than exploratory, areas of focus, and there is an assumption that what to do with the findings will be obvious, even though KAP surveys offer very little explanatory insights into why certain knowledge, attitudes, and practices exist (Launiala, 2009). Although it may be possible to disaggregate data from KAP surveys to understand *critical* dimensions of inequality between different demographics, they have been critiqued for being unreliable (since people try to give 'correct' answers for attitudes and behaviours) and for under-recognizing the challenges of translation and interpretation into local languages (Launiala, 2009). Finally, KAP surveys are not particularly useful for understanding *complicated* and *complex* situations, since they are based on quite a simple theory of change – this theory is that a lack of knowledge is the main factor for attitudes, which are the main factor for behaviour.

In response to this critique, the remainder of the chapter provides an innovative participatory alternative approach to KAP surveys in support of behaviour change communication in the form of community-based action research. This was pioneered in work with UNICEF Tanzania as an alternative to KAP surveys in response to violence against children.

Building a case for a participatory alternative in research for social change

The critique above highlights that simply gaining knowledge about attitudes and practices might help understand current attitudes and behaviours but will have little effect on challenging the complex socio-cultural contexts that give rise to violence. The popular statement from Einstein that 'we cannot solve our problems with the same minds we used to create them' seems relevant here. This means that in order to bring about change we need to change mindsets. Changing mindsets involves an active process of critical questioning of attitudes and practices and finding alternatives. This requires those concerned finding new ways in which to think and act – in essence, an active 'learning approach' (Tilbury, 2007). Schratz and Walker (1995) argue that '[p]articipation in research for social change needs to involve a total human experience for all participants'. Social change therefore needs to involve a *transformational learning* process (Gaventa, 2004) that actively involves individuals and communities, and that challenges and changes norms and values that are at the core of daily practices. The C4D principles outlined above provide a useful contribution in thinking about the wider components of a 'learning for change' approach. Self-determination is a fundamental driver for human beings. Being told to change will frequently be met with resistance. In contrast, when people learn and realize experientially the need for change they are more likely to be motivated to change as a result of a heightened awareness about an issue after reflecting critically on attitudes and practices and becoming aware that new choices and actions are possible. (Social) learning is therefore central to social and behaviour change and necessitates the active engagement of community members in critically reflecting on behaviours, attitudes, and practices.

There is an established tradition of post-positivist participative approaches to learning and change; these are reflected in approaches such as participatory action research (PAR), participatory appraisal, rapid rural appraisal, cooperative inquiry, whole system action inquiry, and so on (see, for example, Kindon et al., 2007; Reason and Bradbury, 2013). Paradoxically, these have been frequently rehearsed in the 'development' sector championed by the likes of Chambers (1997), Cornwall and Coelho (2007), Johnson et al. (1998), and Burns and Worsley (2015). Underlying these approaches are some fundamental principles that set them apart from more conventional approaches to research and programming and that resonate with the C4D framework. These include:

- active participation of community stakeholders working together to resolve problems;
- collectively developing a better/holistic understanding of the problem at hand as a basis for change;
- centrality of 'learning' rooted in reflection, dialogue, and inquiry in response to stories and experiences in everyday lived realities;
- a focus on critical questioning of taken-for-granted assumptions underlying systems and practices with a view to bringing about change and developing alternatives;
- participants building capacity for change and developing a sense of their own power (empowerment) to bring about change as a result of 'new' knowledge and a heightened awareness of the problem at hand from which new strategies for change can emerge;
- outcomes that have value for those involved.

PAR (and its variants) offers an alternative approach to research that actively involves community members and other stakeholders as co-researchers in understanding and responding to the issues at hand. As Reason (1988) states:

'the process is simple. It is about people working together to change their world.' In this sense it can be understood as a transformational and collaborative process of (social) learning for change that begins with dialogue and sharing stories from experience and evolves through critical reflection on current practices and the creation of 'alternative' strategies for action (Percy-Smith, 2006). Action research as used in this study draws in particular on participatory social learning theory as articulated by Wildemeersch et al. (1998), who conceptualize a process of learning in groups and communities where the emphasis is on harnessing the problem-solving potential of the group. It is focused on action and experience; is critically reflective, meaning that actors question opinions and actions; is cooperative; and is communicative, meaning that dialogue is crucial. Participatory social learning is an 'asset-based approach' involving community stakeholders getting together to find solutions to a common problem that they feel are appropriate. While such a process of action research may involve resources people within the community possess as a form of community self-help (Burns et al., 2004), understanding the wider systemic context and factors that give rise to particular problems may also involve identifying actions that need to happen outside the community.

A key concept running through action research is 'critical reflexivity'. Critical reflexivity is fundamental to action research and refers to the process by which participants locate themselves within the inquiry and remain open to changing what they do as a result of learning and reflection. As Weil (1998) states, action research involves 'problem-centred research involving learning *"with"* not *"on"* people that challenges and changes individuals and the systems and practices of which they are part'. The ideal of PAR is for those concerned to self-organize in a process of learning for change (Reason, 1988). In reality, however, this rarely happens. Instead, the researcher or community development practitioner acts as a facilitator for community learning for change.

The evolution and design of a community-based action research project to respond to VAC

In 2014, the University of Huddersfield was invited by UNICEF Tanzania in collaboration with the Government of Tanzania to undertake a KAP study to understand the socio-cultural drivers of VAC as a basis for creating a protective environment for children. This was to involve focus groups and a KAP survey in 10 regions across Tanzania and Zanzibar. An inception phase included undertaking initial focus groups with children, parents, community leaders, and professionals. It became clear from these preliminary explorations that parents and children do not normally feel able to talk about violence against children. At the same time, for a majority of participants, there was a clear message that socio-cultural practices that give rise to violence are not acceptable and should be challenged. It also became evident that UNICEF, in collaboration with the government, which is a signatory to the Convention on the Rights of the Child, had a stated commitment to influence change in communities. As a result, the researchers proposed rethinking the study methodology using an action research approach to actively engage community members in exploring, and critically reflecting on, the socio-cultural factors (values, attitudes, and assumptions) that underpin VAC and, by gaining a better understanding of the issues at play, to collectively explore possibilities for change.

In developing a revised action research approach, there was a number of considerations. First, given that this was a piece of commissioned research with outcomes in the form of 'new knowledge' expected, it was not realistic to let the process evolve organically out of community dialogue. Instead, the architecture of the process was prescribed by the UK research lead in collaboration with a national university in Tanzania. Second, this is a 'new' approach for local researchers and community members, so the process had to be simplified. Third, because UNICEF wanted some kind of benchmark of knowledge, attitudes, and practices in the community, this was factored in to the process in the form of a participatory appraisal process. What resulted was a form of community-based action research tailored to a commissioned research process.

The design of the approach involved two main phases. In the first instance, focus groups were undertaken with children, parents, community leaders, and professionals to explore socio-cultural dynamics in relation to violence against children. But for change to happen it was important to also engage participants in reflection and dialogue in response to prevailing attitudes and practices. Learning from this phase was then used to provide the focus for the community action research process in phase two. This phase involved two parts: participatory research with children and community action research with adult community members. A total of 2,016 participants, including children aged 13–17, were involved in the project.

The inclusion of children as citizens in community participatory processes ideally involves children alongside adults in an intergenerational approach. However, given the culturally framed power differentials at play, the lack of a culture of involving children, and wider ethical considerations, it was deemed of more value to have separate 'spaces' in which to engage children. Participatory research with children in each of the 10 regions was undertaken over two meetings and involved activities including: discussion with children about their understandings of violence and harm and why it happens; community mapping of where they feel safe and unsafe; drawings to capture and discuss children's experiences of VAC; a diary or timeline of a week in a child's life when they feel safe and unsafe; discussions about what causes them to feel vulnerable; children's visions of a protective environment; and messages ('letters') to adults about how they feel about how adults treat children and what they think should change.

The design was for the work with children and young people to be undertaken first in order to feed into the adult action research groups.

Figure 2.1 Supporting the active involvement of young people
Source: Copyright Maria Obel Malila

However, due to time and logistical difficulties, this did not always happen, and some groups were undertaken in parallel.

The community action research process with adults involved three main elements:

1. undertaking a participatory appraisal of attitudes and practices in the community in relation to VAC (see Figure 2.2);
2. facilitated dialogue and reflection in response to participatory appraisal about community attitudes and practices (see Figure 2.3);
3. generating priorities for change involving action planning, including identifying the change needed, who needs to be involved, what community resources can be used, and criteria for monitoring change (see Figure 2.4).

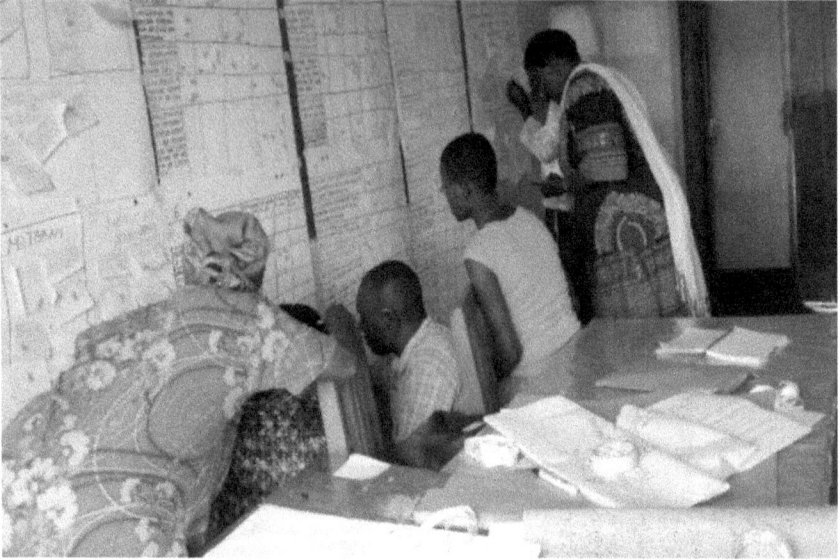

Figure 2.2 Participatory appraisal with adults
Source: Copyright Isabela Warioba

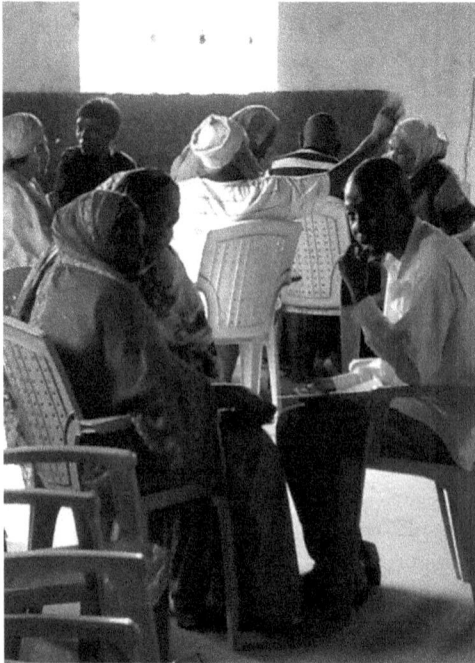

Figure 2.3 Dialogue and reflection in response to participatory appraisal
Source: Copyright Seraphina Bakta

Figure 2.4 Identifying priorities for change
Source: Copyright Barry Percy-Smith

Running through the whole process was a local community reference group set up in each study location to engage local stakeholders (including parents, children, community members, and professionals) at three stages of the research. The purpose of this group was to reflect on the significance of the findings for programming and to develop local ownership and accountability, and to reflect on and support action in response to the learning that emerged from the study. The underlying rationale was that power in relation to the outcomes of the study should rest in the hands of local stakeholders, who would then sustain momentum after the study finished as an 'action-focused' group. This was also a way of developing more of a whole systems approach to change that involved all parts of the system rather than just working with community members.

In addition, national learning workshops (see Figure 2.5) were organized in Tanzania mainland and Zanzibar to bring together key stakeholders including government ministries, professionals (from child protection, community development, police, and criminal justice departments, etc.), NGO representatives, UNICEF staff, children, and academics to reflect on and discuss the implications of the learning from the study to inform policy and practice developments.

Figure 2.5 Engaging with learning from the study at a national stakeholder event
Source: Copyright Barry Percy-Smith

These local and national 'forums' are essentially focused on constructing and developing commitment for 'action'. This involves opening up possibilities for action and change in communities, in local services and municipalities, and in policy at national government level. In an ideal context, in such a study, there would be time to implement changes and evaluate them in the context of a longer cycle of action research. This was not possible, however, within the timeline of this project.

The whole process can be summarized graphically as shown in Figure 2.6.

Reflections on the process and outcomes of using community action research in response to VAC

One of the tensions in doing action research is between the rhetorics and realities of praxis (Weil, 1998). There are a number of issues here. First, as with any piece of commissioned research, this study had a finite limit on time and resources. In reality, researchers found that they needed more time to work with community members to build relationships and trust, and to ensure sufficient time for the community action research process to happen. Ideally, rather than one community workshop per region there would be a series of meetings to enable cycles of dialogue and inquiry to develop over time. Social issues such as VAC are complex and sensitive and need time for

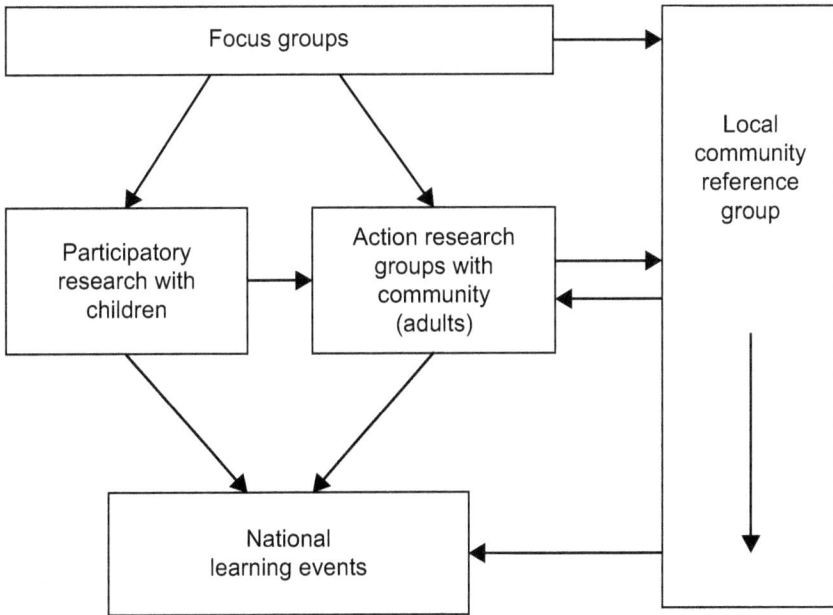

Figure 2.6 A whole system action research process

participants to explore and critically question values and practices as part of a transformational learning or deep inquiry process to inform change. Projects therefore need to include sufficient time for actions to be implemented and in turn evaluated to do justice to the process. When time-limited research is commissioned, as with this project, it is important for the programme partners to pick up the project and its findings, and to follow through with practical action with stakeholders. In this project, there was a clear message to the communities that the findings will inform the development of the communication programme to address violence against women and children and the child protection system. Yet participants on the ground may be left feeling that this is just another research project that results in nothing happening, a concern expressed by participants.

Second, PAR is normally considered to be initiated by community members. In contrast, this process was clearly driven by UNICEF and in danger of becoming another example of the tyranny of participation that Cooke and Kothari (2001) discuss. Yet within this context there was significant value in adopting this approach, as community participants had an opportunity to be involved actively in inquiry, rather than just as respondents. The community-based action research involved providing a safe space for participants to have an opportunity to voice views and perspectives, hear the opinions of others, and engage in dialogue in ways that might otherwise not be possible. By including participatory appraisal into the process, local leaders and parents were supported in undertaking 'self-assessment' to provide a more informed basis for discussion and for participants themselves to perceive the socio-cultural drivers and responses to violence.

Third, one of the arguments for encouraging UNICEF to adopt this approach was that it has a better chance than KAP surveys at building capacity in communities. Indeed, the learning that can take place within an action research process can be quite revelatory and transformative, in terms of new insights and participants having their thinking and practice challenged. See, for example, the following reflections from participants.

> Every child experienced some kind of violence ... we are still doing violence to children without knowing we are denying their rights. This kind of discussion needs to be conducted ... as it acts as an eye opener. (Community member)

> We did what we did in good intention, but we were actually abusing our children. The community need to be sensitized on these practices and I will be at the frontier of correcting what we used to do. (Father)

> This workshop has changed me a lot, simply because there were some behaviour and action I used to do to children and I never recognize them as VAC, so it made me change and to be attracted to change others. (Adult professional)

However, while there are identifiable, tangible benefits such as these, building the capacity for systems and practices to change takes longer than is possible within the timescale of a single project and depends on the buy-in of stake-holders. Projects need continuity of funding, beyond short-term funding cycles, to build on and sustain the momentum of learning and change initiatives around specific issues. Action research is a 'new' approach for many professionals, national policy leads, researchers, and community members alike, and it is unrealistic for those concerned to be able to realize the benefits from the process in such a short timescale. Hence, in the national learning events, despite the sessions being set up to facilitate the engagement of participants in reflection and dialogue in response to learning from the project, many of the participants didn't take up this opportunity, instead assuming a role that focused on verifying findings. Similarly, at a local level, while participants can readily express their views and experiences, they are not predisposed to actively engage as change agents. Indeed, the idea of speaking out and 'challenging thinking and practice' can be countercultural in some contexts.

Fourth, participants have different needs. In this project, some participants had low levels of literacy, and while measures were put in place to support them, this affected their ability to take part and increased the time needed to run the process. The use of visuals is one way of getting around this, although this may result in variable interpretation by different participants.

Fifth, it is important to create a flexible space for emergence. As a result of working with complexity, the inquiry process can bring to the fore other issues at play that are important in their own right, such as gender equality and the right of the child to participate in decision making. For example, in one study area, the project engaged women and men separately for ethical reasons to ensure that women had enough space for discussion, yet participants argued that bringing men and women together was important in challenging gender stereotypes, which itself is part of the issue of violence against children.

Finally, action research is not just a research method but is a whole system approach to learning for change. That means that it is as much about action and change as it is about learning and generating new knowledge with a view to bringing about change. It can therefore be seen as a research process that is action focused as well as a process of change informed by learning. This means that it can be used as an approach to programming as well as a form of research, to generate new learning.

Having highlighted some of the limitations and challenges with using action research, it is important to acknowledge the value of such an approach, however humbly. A frequent contestation from community members is of being 'done to', or of being researched and then having 'solutions' imposed that they have not been part of developing. One of the major strengths of this approach is that it goes beyond simply collecting data, to enable participants to use that data to make decisions about change and to engage in conversations to challenge assumptions and practices. In this way, it provides opportunities for extending ownership and self-determination to local community stakeholders as agents of change in their own right. In doing this, there are a number of more specific merits to this approach.

In focusing on the centrality of communication, dialogue, and interaction in action research, one of the key advantages of this approach is that it creates spaces for speaking the unspoken and for dialogue and critical questioning. This in itself has value in breaking the conservatism of cultural practices and in challenging assumptions and perceptions of powerlessness. Moreover, in bringing people together around issues of mutual concern, solidarity can be developed that enables community capacity building and in turn can help sustain momentum for change through in-depth collaborative action inquiry, something that is less likely with conventional research methods. Indeed, irrespective of responses to the issue at hand, the experience of going through an action research process in itself provides a valuable learning opportunity for individuals and communities. In particular, this approach enabled participants to bring to the surface some of the complex dynamics, paradoxes, and contradictions that underpin VAC and that can inform strategies for change without resorting to simple solutions. Examples include the following:

- Through the action inquiry process, participants were able to critically reflect on the extent to which taken-for-granted socio-cultural norms contribute to VAC in their own context.
- Reflection and dialogue concerned the way in which beating continues under the guise of good upbringing, despite children saying that it causes them to feel fearful, resentful, and unloved.

- Change needs to be owned and driven by the community (or communities), but VAC is part of a wider culture of fear and silence that reinforces the status quo, prevents values and practices being questioned, and undermines individual agency. Providing safe spaces to hear the unspoken views of women and children can be pivotal in taking steps towards change.
- The response to VAC has to go beyond dealing with just the immediate issues; instead, it needs to address underlying socio-cultural norms rooted in patriarchy and gender roles and embodied in everyday socio-cultural practices.
- It is important to bring to the surface the extent to which poverty is both a cause and an effect of violence against children. The message to all involved in child protection is therefore that the economic empowerment of communities and the realization of social, economic, and cultural rights are imperative if children are to be protected from all forms of violence.
- The way in which professionals normally seen as dependable 'pillars of society' (such as teachers, police, and the courts) are part of the problem has to be exposed. Their position gives rise to a reluctance to report VAC, which further reinforces cultures of patriarchy and subservience. At the same time, community lore exerts a more powerful influence than judicial law on the way children are treated.

The significance of these 'findings' is not simply that they fill the gaps in knowledge that KAP surveys might seek to address; rather, they engage community participants and stakeholders in a learning process, creating a sense of ownership, responsibility, and empowerment not only to understand the problem, but through a deeper level of inquiry, to also propose solutions and signal ways forward to address these problems.

For possibilities of change to be maximized, it is imperative for initiatives at community level to be mirrored and supported by developments in policy, legislation, and services. For example, building capacity for change in communities can be of limited value if the police and criminal justice system routinely fail to bring perpetrators of VAC to justice. Following the precepts of realist evaluation approaches (Pawson and Tilley, 1997), for a change mechanism (action research) to be effective in bringing about a particular outcome (reduction of violence against children), it is necessary to ensure that appropriate contextual conditions (supportive public services) are in place. Hence, in connection with VAC, addressing systemic corruption and ineffectiveness in the courts and police is essential in providing a moral imperative, precedent, and stimulus for social action and change to happen. Also, understanding community power structures and social dynamics will strengthen the linkages between the community and the judicial system.

Monitoring and evaluation are central to programming initiatives, and are normally devised by external organizations in line with programming objectives. Yet, with a participatory action research approach, criteria and indicators for monitoring and assessment are developed in relation to actions for change that are identified in the action research process, based on what is meaningful and realistic for partner communities, who in turn can then be involved in participatory monitoring and evaluation.

Conclusions

The participatory action research approach in this project was used to fill the research gap in the previous prevalence study, by involving communities in exploring their socio-cultural values and practices in relation to VAC. In the process, the harmful social practices affecting children were challenged and possible drivers of positive change identified. Emphasis was placed on learning from a diversity of views and experiences of community members who were purposively recruited from a wide range of stakeholders. The findings from the PAR yielded critical insights into the social-cultural context of violence against children and women; this has relevance across various sectors from parenting programmes and social welfare to the judicial system, education, and national-level policies and law reforms.

The community dialogue with various groups, including women, men, children, community leaders, and professionals, illuminated the social construct of violence and the intersection between socio-cultural norms (i.e. regarding physical punishment and local values of discipline), gender norms (including masculinity), and structural factors such as family poverty, lack of trust in the child protection systems, and parental stress. Powerful paradoxes and contradictions emerged, such as perceptions of physical punishment, showing the intergenerational divide between parents' and children's views. These findings have provided a critical body of knowledge in the development of child protection systems that are grounded and well informed by the socio-cultural context of Tanzania. Central to the community action research process was the 'critically reflexive learning' that occurred with participants through a heightened sense of empowerment. This was a result of the learning process community members went through, generating new insights and awareness while breaking the culture of silence with regard to collective community discussion about VAC and specifically sexual violence.

This chapter has shared some important innovations that go to the heart of some of the limitations of KAPs and provides an innovative participatory, learning-based alternative to C4D. In doing so it exemplifies the Evaluating C4D framework (Lennie and Tacchi, 2013) set out earlier, highlighting the central importance of participatory approaches to dialogue and inquiry rooted in situated socio-cultural contexts. It involves the adoption of a critical and holistic approach to social learning in which participants hear different perspectives, question assumptions and practices, and reflect on actions and choices in light of that community-based learning. This learning involves paying attention to the dynamics and underlying relationships, including identifying contradictions and paradoxes that play out between the rhetoric of social norms and values and the realities in practice. Most significantly, the principles of the community-based action research discussed here provide a participatory alternative not just to KAP surveys but also to programming and development in which communities themselves become actors of social change.

Acknowledgements

The authors would like to thank the community researchers and participants involved in this study, research colleagues at Mzumbe University and University of Huddersfield who contributed to the study, and UNICEF Tanzania and the Tanzanian government for funding the study.

References

Bicchieri, C. and Mercier, H. (2014) 'Norms and beliefs: how change occurs', *Iyyun: The Jerusalem Philosophical Quarterly* 63 (January): 60–82.
Bronfenbrenner, U. (1979) *The Ecology of Human Development*, Harvard University Press, Cambridge MA.
Burns, D. and Worsley, S. (2015) *Navigating Complexity in International Development: Facilitating Sustainable Change at Scale*, Practical Action Publishing, Rugby.
Burns, D. et al. (2004) *Community Self-help*, Palgrave Macmillan, Basingstoke.
Chambers, R. (1997) *Whose Reality Counts? Putting the First Last*, IT Publications, London.
Cleland, J. (1973) 'A critique of KAP studies and some suggestions for their improvement', *Studies in Family Planning* 4 (2): 42–7.
Cooke, B. and Kothari, U. (2001) *Participation: The New Tyranny?*, Zed Books, London.
Cornwall, A. and Coelho, V.S. (2007) *Spaces for Change? The Politics of Citizen Participation in New Democratic Arenas*, Zed Books, London.
Crosson-Tower, C. (2008) *Understanding Child Abuse and Neglect*, Pearson, New York.
Gaventa, J. (2004) 'Towards participatory governance: assessing the transformative possibilities', in S. Hickey and G. Mohan (eds), *Participation from Tyranny to Transformation: Exploring New Approaches to Participation in Development*, Zed Books, London.
Hickey, S. and Mohan, G. (2004) *Participation from Tyranny to Transformation: Exploring New Approaches to Participation in Development*, Zed Books, London.
Hornik, R.C. (2002) 'Public health communication: making sense of contradictory evidence', in R.C. Hornik (ed.), *Public Health Communication: Evidence for Behavior Change*, Lawrence Erlbaum Associates Publishers, Mahwah NJ and London.
Johnson, V. et al. (eds) (1998) *Stepping Forward: Children and Young People's Participation in the Development Process*, IT Publications, London.
Jones, A. (ed.) (2013) *Understanding Child Sexual Abuse: Perspectives from the Caribbean*, Palgrave Macmillan, Basingstoke.

Kemmis, S. (2001) 'Exploring the relevance of critical theory for action research: emancipatory action research in the footsteps of Jürgen Habermas', in P. Reason and H. Bradbury (eds), *The Handbook of Action Research, Participative Inquiry and Practice*, pp. 90–102, Sage, London.

Kindon, S., Pain, R. and Kesby, M. (2007) *Participatory Action Research Approaches and Methods: Connecting People, Participation and Place*, Routledge, Abingdon and New York.

Launiala, A. (2009) 'How much can a KAP survey tell us about people's knowledge, attitudes and practices? Some observations from medical anthropology research on malaria in pregnancy in Malawi', *Anthropology Matters Journal* 11 (1): 1–13.

Lennie, J. and Tacchi, J. (2013) *Evaluating Communication for Development: A Framework for Social Change*, Earthscan/Routledge, New York.

Manyozo, L. (2012) *Media, Communication and Development: Three Approaches*, Sage, London.

Morris, N. (2003) 'A comparative analysis of the diffusion and participatory models in development communication', *Communication Theory* 13 (2): 225–48 <https://doi.org/10.1111/j.1468-2885.2003.tb00290.x>.

Noske-Turner, J. (2020) 'Operationalizing a framework for C4D evaluation', in J. Noske-Turner (ed.), *Communication for Development: An Evaluation Framework in Action*, Practical Action Publishing, Rugby.

Pawson, R. and Tilley, N. (1997) *Realist Evaluation*, Sage, London.

Pelto, P.J. and Pelto, G.H. (1997) 'Studying knowledge, culture, and behavior in applied medical anthropology', *Medical Anthropology Quarterly* 11 (2): 147–63.

Percy-Smith, B. (2006) 'From consultation to social learning in community participation with young people', *Children, Youth and Environments* 16 (2): 153–79.

Percy-Smith, B. et al. (2017) *Report from the Study of Socio-cultural Drivers of Violence and Positive Change in Tanzania*, UNICEF Tanzania and University of Huddersfield (unpublished).

Portela de Souza, P. (2010) 'Is acceptance of child labour a social norm in Bangladesh?', unpublished paper, UNICEF/University of Pennsylvania.

Reason, P. (1988) *Human Inquiry in Action: Developments in New Paradigm Research*, Sage, London.

Reason, P. and Bradbury, H. (eds) (2013) *Handbook of Action Research*, 2nd edn, Sage, London.

Schopper, D., Doussantousse, S. and Orav, J. (1993) 'Sexual behaviors relevant to HIV transmission in a rural African population: how much can a KAP survey tell us?', *Social Science and Medicine* 37 (3): 401–12.

Schratz, B. and Walker, R. (1995) *Research as Social Change: New Opportunities for Qualitative Research*, Routledge, London.

Scott, M. (2014) *Media and Development*, Zed Books, London.

Sparks, C. (2007) *Globalization, Development and the Mass Media*, Sage, London.

Tilbury, D. (2007) 'Learning-based change for sustainability: perspectives and pathways', in A.E.J. Wals (ed.), *Social Learning: Towards a Sustainable World*, pp. 117–32, Wageningen Publishers, Wageningen.

UN (2006) *General Assembly Report of the Independent Expert for the United Nations Study on Violence against Children*, United Nations (UN), New York.

UNICEF Tanzania, Division of Violence Prevention, National Center for Injury Prevention and Control, Centres for Disease Control and Prevention, and Muhimbili University of Health and Allied Sciences (UNICEF, CDC, MUHAS) (2011) *Violence against Children in Tanzania: Findings from a National Survey, 2009*, United Republic of Tanzania, Dar es Salaam.

Weil, S. (1998) 'Rhetorics and realities in public service organisations: systemic practice and organisational learning as Critically Reflexive Action Research (CRAR)', *Systemic Practice and Action Research* 11: 37–61.

Wildemeersch, D., Jansen, T. and Vandenabeele, J. (1998) 'Social learning: a new perspective on learning in participatory systems', *Studies in Continuing Education* 20: 251–65.

Author biographies

Barry Percy-Smith is Professor of Childhood, Youth and Participatory Practice at the University of Huddersfield, UK. He has extensive experience as an action researcher in research, evaluation, and development projects with children, young people, and practitioners in a wide range of public-sector and community contexts.

Seraphina Msengi Bakta is a lecturer and researcher in the Faculty of Law, Mzumbe University, Tanzania, specializing in child rights. She is also an advocate of the High Court of Tanzania.

Jessica Noske-Turner is a lecturer in Media and Creative Industries, Loughborough University London. From 2014 to 2017 she was a postdoctoral fellow at RMIT University, contributing to the *Evaluating C4D: Supporting Adaptive and Accountable Development* research project.

Georgina Mtenga is a practitioner in the field of social and behaviour change communication, working with UNICEF as Communication for Development Specialist in the Yemen (formerly Tanzania) Country Office.

Patricia Portela Souza is the Deputy Representative for UNICEF Angola. In her 21 years of experience in UNICEF she has been the C4D Regional Adviser for the Eastern and Southern African Regional Office and a C4D specialist in Brazil, Mozambique, and Bangladesh and at UNICEF HQ in New York.

CHAPTER 3

Finding and creating opportunities for participatory approaches to RM&E in Vietnam

Tran Phuong-Anh, Jessica Noske-Turner and Ho Anh Tung

Definitions of Communication for Development (C4D) emphasize inclusive processes of participation and horizontal dialogue. Such concepts, however, are quite foreign in the context of the very centralized, hierarchical government structures in Vietnam. This context posed significant challenges when seeking to apply participatory approaches and resources in keeping with the Evaluating C4D framework. This chapter reflects on the challenges of implementing participatory approaches in Vietnam, paying attention to instances where participatory approaches have successfully been introduced through working directly with government systems. While recognizing the need to adapt thinking about participation, with the experience drawn from UNICEF Vietnam Country Office and other local stakeholders, the chapter argues that it is important to persist with culturally appropriate efforts to encourage more participatory approaches to research, monitoring, and evaluation.

Keywords: Communication for Development; evaluation; participatory; research; Vietnam

Introduction

There is a wide consensus on the importance and value of participatory communication approaches in the Communication for Development (C4D) literature. Participation and communication have been described as two sides of the same coin (Fraser and Restrepo-Estrada, 1998), and many others have promoted listening, dialogue, and collective action, distinguishing these approaches from the more diffusionist and unidirectional approaches that are associated with the modernization paradigm (Waisbord, 2001; Quarry and Ramírez, 2009; Morris, 2003; Melkote, 2003). These notions of participatory communication have deep historical roots originating from various Southern contexts, including the Latin American, Southern African, Filipino/Los Baños, and Indian schools of thought informing C4D approaches (Manyozo, 2012). Freirian dialogical approaches that seek to reveal oppressions and foster

http://dx.doi.org/10.3362/9781780449968.003

critical consciousness have become particularly important (Manyozo, 2017; Tufte, 2017; Thomas and van de Fliert, 2014). It was on the basis of this commitment to participation as core to C4D that Lennie and Tacchi (2013) argued that participation was a foundational principle of their framework for evaluating C4D.

While participatory approaches are broadly promoted as ideal practice, in this chapter we ask: Is there a danger in universalizing expectations and procedures for participation? While it is true that participatory approaches emerged from thinking and practice originating from the Global South, what happens when these concepts travel and are transferred to other contexts, with different histories, knowledges, and cultural contexts? How do we need to rethink assumptions about participation to make practices culturally appropriate and effective, and so that different forms of participation can be recognized?

This chapter reflects on our participatory action research in Vietnam as part of the Evaluating C4D project, a partnership between university researchers and UNICEF C4D. UNICEF Vietnam was the first country office to actively engage in the project. The university-based researchers visited Hanoi for the 'scoping research' in February 2015, at which time it was agreed that we would focus on UNICEF's global End Violence Against Children (EVAC) initiatives. The C4D team (led by Tran Phuong-Anh as the specialist with a portfolio covering child protection C4D) were working with the Child Protection team and their government counterparts in the Ministry of Labour, Invalids, and Social Affairs (MOLISA) and were in the process of recruiting a consultant to undertake an evaluation of a localized EVAC communication campaign. The timing and relationships with key stakeholders made it a valuable opportunity to collaborate, trial new approaches, and critically reflect on our actions. In June 2015, Ho Anh Tung joined the team as a Hanoi-based, full-time research assistant on the project. Late in 2015 we collaborated with the Vietnamese consultant commissioned to undertake the assessment of the campaign. This experience, together with experiences in other offices, informed the first draft of practical resources for evaluating C4D in UNICEF based on the framework established by Lennie and Tacchi (2013). In May 2016 we had an opportunity to trial the draft resources, since UNICEF C4D was in the process of supporting MOLISA to develop the next phase of the EVAC programme, including designing an evaluation framework.

In this chapter we reflect on these efforts to use learning-based and participatory evaluation approaches in Vietnam. We reflect on what our action research revealed about the assumptions and expectations, and the ways we might need to rethink what participation means and how to apply it in a context such as Vietnam. We discuss the historical and cultural contexts influencing approaches to communication, C4D, and evaluation, and how participatory approaches can and have been adapted to better respond to these contexts.

Concepts of participation in a global context

There is widespread agreement that participatory approaches to communication and development ought to be core to practice (Chambers, 1983, 2012; Manyozo, 2017). In a participatory approach, local people have a right to be actively and genuinely involved in defining and determining their own development. Communication initiatives may include information sharing, but they should also seek to raise people's awareness of the contexts and structures, and opportunities to take collective action and create social change (Freire, 2000; Tufte, 2017; Manyozo, 2017; Thomas and van de Fliert, 2014). Although participatory approaches today are often strongly associated with Latin American schools of thought, participatory approaches have emerged from within a number of distinctive cultures in the Asian region, including from the Philippines (Quebral, 1976; Manyozo, 2006) and India (Dutta, 2011), and with more recent reflections on concepts of participation in Thailand (Servaes, 2000; Supadhiloke, 2013). Despite some calls for cultural interpretation (for example, to Asian or collectivist values), the commitment to inclusive participation by these scholars is strongly maintained.

As a consequence of this consensus, participatory evaluation approaches are strongly advocated in C4D. This enables stakeholders and communities concerned to define their own visions for development, set criteria for what success looks like, and learn and adapt their efforts empowered by the knowledge generated through their evaluations (Lennie and Tacchi, 2013; Noske-Turner, 2017; Thomas and van de Fliert, 2014). Participatory evaluation has a long history. It first emerged in the 1960s and 1970s in response to dissatisfaction with the 'mechanistic and insensitive' approaches that dominated at the time (Fitzpatrick et al., 2004: 130–1). At their heart, participatory evaluation approaches seek to address the power asymmetries in knowledge and decision making in development (Armytage, 2011: 272). Participatory evaluation is defined according to the values of participant ownership, inclusiveness, and engagement, rather than by any specific methods (Chouinard, 2013: 242).

While there is agreement on the importance of participatory approaches, often there are limitations on the extent to which claims to use bottom-up, participatory approaches are actually reflected in the practice of development, communication, and evaluation (Cornwall and Brock, 2005; White, 1996). The main barriers identified in the literature are the bureaucratic structures of development that entrench top-down, pre-planned, and upward accountability to donors rather than citizens (Waisbord, 2008; Lennie and Tacchi, 2013; Wilkins, 2018).

Concepts of participation and communication in the Vietnam context

There is comparatively little literature specifically dealing with participatory approaches in communication, development, and evaluation in Vietnam, but the work by international and Vietnamese scholars exploring the concept of participation in this context suggests that globally dominant ideas of participation cannot simply be transplanted into the Vietnam context. Explorations of Vietnamese concepts of participation need to be understood in a cultural context.

In particular, Confucianism has remained the prevailing influence on thinking about communication in Vietnam. Confucian qualities of bureaucratic hierarchy, ideological conformity, and an emphasis on formal ideologies have been the operative principles of the Vietnamese government's communicative practices (Tung Hieu, 2016). Historical ways of organizing are also significant. In Vietnam's post-revolutionary history, 'citizen participation' is often rooted in the realm of the mass mobilization (*dân vận*) of peasants and workers in support of the state (McElwee and Ha, 2006). In other words, mass organizations (*các đoàn thể*) led by the Vietnam Fatherland Front have played a key role in 'representation' (considered as a form of participation) and as 'the main vehicle through which citizens gain access to participation in the country's socio-political context' (McElwee and Ha, 2006: 7).

In terms of approaches to communication, globally established concepts relating to C4D do not have a high profile in Vietnam, and indeed do not always harmonize with the traditional communication approaches of the country, which are generally quite hierarchical and centralized, with significant influences from this Confucian culture. Throughout recent history, the foundation of 'communication' in Vietnam, as it had been conceived historically, was that it was not meant to communicate, but rather to inform. Instead, historically, Information, Education, and Communication (IEC), which is a comparatively top-down, message-driven approach, has been used more commonly. In the past, IEC was a tightly regulated process with coordinated action within government-guided ideological principles (Laverack and Huy Dap, 2003). IEC typically uses mass communication media including television, radio, print materials (such as posters, leaflets, and brochures), and public announcement loudspeaker systems (although in 2017 the loudspeaker systems were switched off in urban areas). These approaches were used to reach a large audience quickly and conveniently.

There are a few instances of a shift away from vertically imposed and rigid model of 'information delivery' from governmental stakeholders. This can usually be credited to long-term partnerships with international development agencies (including UNICEF and others) that provide training on other methods of communication. In urban areas, digital communication platforms, reaching 44 per cent of the Vietnamese population (Abuza, 2015), have also provided an impetus for the government to shift its IEC focus and use government websites and social media portals to communicate and interact in a less one-way direction. However, in the context of the continuing top-down structure, the majority of decisions about communication activities are made at the ministry (national) level across sectors. This creates barriers to participatory planning of communication on the subnational level, as well as the community level.

In relation to participation by children and adolescents, the Government of Vietnam was the second in the world to ratify the UN Convention on the Rights of the Child in 1990. One year later in 1991, the first and the most comprehensive law on children – the Law on Protection, Care, and Education of Children – was developed, serving as an important legal framework. Later, the Vietnam 2013 Constitution (under Article 37) articulated that children have the right to participate in all matters relating to their lives. While a number of laws give children a legal voice in particular issues affecting their lives, overall the laws relating to children's right to participation are somewhat scattered (UNICEF Vietnam, 2010). Further, while there have been gains made in terms of constitutional and legal requirements for participation, the implementation is less clear. An assessment study (UNICEF Vietnam, 2014) identified seven key factors constraining child participation in Vietnam including: 1) unclear definition of child participation; 2) absence of regulations on the scope of child participation (for example in the context of family, communities, schools, and other settings); 3) lack of guidance for implementation of child participation activities; 4) child participation has not been made compulsory – it is mainly dependent on the commitment of individual local leaders; 5) limited awareness of the importance or benefit of child participation among children, parents, community leaders, and other stakeholders; 6) absence of a formal mechanism for promoting and coordinating child participation; and 7) limited capacity to undertake child participation activities among adults working on and with children.

The use of participatory monitoring and evaluation approaches in the Vietnam context is similarly constrained, with a number of studies reflecting on challenges. Minh, Larsen, and Neef (2010) found that it was possible to introduce different approaches to participation that shift the conventional hierarchical systems of authority and top-down training, but only through a slow and adaptive process. Quaghebeur, Masschelein, and Nguyen (2004) found contradictions in the intention of participatory approaches to reverse power structures, where it paradoxically enforced a series of different hierarchies and Western-centric notions of individualism. On the other hand, Nicetic and van de Fliert concluded that it was crucial that international and Vietnamese partners co-develop a 'locally suitable collaborative mechanism' by listening and learning from each other rather than imposing international concepts of participation (2014: 67).

Reflections on efforts to introduce participatory evaluation approaches

During the scoping research workshops (held in February 2015 at the UNICEF Vietnam Hanoi Office), the UNICEF C4D and Child Protection teams and the university research team established a joint goal to use the Evaluating C4D framework with a priority focus on three principles: participatory, learning-based, and realistic. In particular, it was noted that while

MOLISA (the national-level ministry with responsibility for child protection) and the relevant provincial-level Departments of Labour, Invalids, and Social Affairs (DOLISAs) are already quite actively involved in programmes, there was a desire within the UNICEF C4D and Child Protection teams to more actively engage with children, schools, parents, and teachers in higher levels of participation.

Two opportunities emerged to seek to incorporate participatory approaches in action. These were: 1) an assessment of the EVAC campaign; and 2) a workshop to design an evaluation framework, which was intended to be both collaboratively developed and to incorporate participation within the design over the programme period.

The EVAC campaign assessment

The EVAC campaign assessment was the first opportunity to collaborate in an action research way on a specific evaluation task. A local consultant was commissioned to undertake the assessment for MOLISA and UNICEF, and the project's research assistant, Ho Anh Tung, collaborated with the consultant. Our research objective was to use the action research opportunity to learn about the practice and context of doing evaluations in the context of UNICEF C4D, with a 'light-touch' approach to intervening with alternative evaluation approaches only if and when opportunities arose. After the assessment was complete, the authors of this chapter undertook an 'After Action Review',[1] which informs the analysis in this section.

The action research process began with co-developing the terms of reference (TOR), through which we sought to highlight the learning-based and formative objectives of the assessment in the TOR's evaluation questions. Second, in addition to a set of quite typical quantitative and qualitative evaluation methods (a desk review of campaign materials), we listed critical listening and feedback sessions (CLFS) as a suggested method. In early meetings with the consultant, we also introduced 'communicative ecology mapping' as a suggested method. CLFS[2] and communicative ecology mapping[3] are engaging and interactive methods that can be used as part of a broader participatory approach; however, in this context they were proposed as interactive researcher-led methods. They were imagined to enable opportunities for enhanced levels of engagement for children and parents in the assessment process.

In practice, as the assessment evolved, there was a stronger focus on assessing the campaign against the programme objectives (rather than the more formatively oriented evaluation questions), which led to a more summative assessment. In addition, it seemed that the consultant was not convinced by the less traditional methods of CLFS and communicative ecology mapping proposed by our research team. Ultimately, it was one of the authors (Ho Anh Tung), in his capacity as the research assistant, who put them into practice in small-scale ways. The combination of these factors meant that a good and useful assessment was produced, but it was one that was fairly typical in terms of approach. We did not have an opportunity to ask the consultant for reflections, but in our reflection processes we identified that a tight budget and the consequent need to scale back the scope of work, coupled with concerns about the efficiency of using the less familiar methods, may have been some reasons for this.

It is also useful to reflect on the experience of trialling these more interactive methods in Vietnam as part of the household interviews. CLFS, in which a video or other media is shown to participants, inviting their interpretations and ideas on how it could be improved, worked quite well, especially with adults. Carrying out the assessment one year after the communication campaign posed various difficulties to the team as well as the participants in recalling past content. CLFS helped to partially overcome this limitation, since it involves a process of showing participants videos and communication materials from the campaign for open-ended feedback. From their feedback, the report could present analysis of the interviewees' perspectives. A recurrent comment was about the discordance between the imagery used in the video and the local context. In the opinion of participants who resided in the mountainous areas of Vietnam, images presented in the video were adapted for city dwellers. Rural residents were less familiar with many concepts shown – e.g. shoe-shining as a symbol for child labour – that were recognized by urbanites. Tailor-made versions or more contextualized materials were therefore suggested to facilitate understanding of the target audience groups.

Communicative ecology mapping, in which participants visually map the information and communicative structures and practices in their everyday lives, was more challenging. It worked well in only two cases (out of the four household visits where it was used) where the children participating were more outgoing. For shy children, there was not enough time to build rapport. On the other hand, the method revealed that the children (especially those in urban areas) live in a media-rich environment with access to multiple devices (phones and tablets). The use of the communicative ecology approach was also enabled through the research assistant's observations and field notes on the presence of communication spaces and technologies in the field sites, such as loudspeakers and school noticeboards. He noted, for example, that sometimes a household practice or their access to communication technologies was different from what was reported in the government stakeholder interviews.

Interestingly, the data from the CLFS and communicative ecology mapping were added to the report after the stakeholder feedback meeting involving the MOLISA partners on the first draft, at which several gaps were noted. This indicates that, although challenging, these two methods generated findings that were more useful and usable, since they responded better to the formative objectives motivating the evaluation.

Evaluation framework design workshop

The second opportunity for collaborative action with a view to using the Evaluating C4D framework approach came the following year. MOLISA, with technical support from UNICEF, needed to develop a monitoring and evaluation (M&E) framework for the forthcoming five-year period relating to the communication aspects of the National Programme for Child Protection. This came at a time when the research team was in the early stages of developing outlines and drafts for a 'C4D M&E guide'. At this early stage it was modelled on the BetterEvaluation Manager's Guide. Informed by this and other experiences of trialling the resources, it eventually evolved into what is now the Evaluating C4D Resource Hub.

The intention was to trial some of the key resources in progress over three half-day workshops. The topics included: 1) stakeholder mapping; 2) establishing decision-making processes; 3) theory of change; 4) exploring simple/complicated/complex aspects of the programme; 5) establishing the scope of the M&E; and 6) identifying the key M&E questions. All three authors were involved in the workshops, and other members of the research team were on hand remotely to debrief and advise between sessions.

A number of not uncommon challenges arose immediately. On the first day it turned out that none of the key people from MOLISA were available for the full schedule, and due to other unavoidable meetings they requested that the workshops be condensed into two short meetings (which would have different participants present in each). This had immediate and significant impacts on the quality of the workshops: there simply was not time for all the processes we had planned, and, with different people present for different meetings, it was hard to develop a sense of collaborative progress towards an M&E plan. The situation was less than optimal for testing the resources, but since time constraints are one of the most common challenges to using participatory approaches, it was perhaps a very real-world test.

There were two significant insights from this workshop that contribute in particular to our understanding of the feasibility of participatory approaches in the Vietnamese context. The first emerged through the stakeholder mapping process. For one of the (non-Vietnamese) authors (Noske-Turner), the stakeholder mapping exercise, together with the activity to examine decision-making processes, led to a revelatory level of understanding about the implications of hierarchical cultures and tensions within participatory approaches. The stakeholder mapping detailed the four distinct levels of stakeholders: national, provincial, and district, with the commune level being identified as the community level. MOLISA, which takes a leading role on child protection plans, typically seeks inputs from other relevant national-level ministries (such as the Ministries for Education, Health, Justice, etc.) to develop a plan. This plan is then taken for consultation in provincial-level departments, led by the DOLISA, while the cross-sectoral work is coordinated through a Child Protection Working Committee, which is established in each province. DOLISAs adapt the plans to their context, and the plans are then shared with the BOLISAs (the district-level Bureaus for Labour, Invalids, and Social Affairs), and then at the commune level. At the lowest level is a network of Child Protection Collaborators, who are the implementers. They are tasked to function as the connection between the families and households and the local administrative agencies for issues related to child protection, and they report to the Commune People's Committee. On our stakeholder map, all the arrows of communication pointed first horizontally and then downwards through the hierarchy, with only monitoring data being identified as officially filtering back up through each level of the hierarchy. Suggestions by Noske-Turner to create feedback loops to directly involve Child Protection Collaborators (who, from her perspective, seemed to be crucial stakeholders given their role in and knowledge about implementation) in some planning and review processes was met with confusion. Opportunities to engage and involve children and parents were not something that was realistically being considered in this context either.

The stakeholder mapping was intended as a precursor to a process of establishing decision-making processes for different kinds of decisions. The resources were intended to prompt discussions about how to involve the critical stakeholders in decision-making processes, and this helps support participatory M&E. The resources presented included a grid setting out different types of decisions against the stakeholders across the top, with space to describe how they are involved (consulted, informed, discuss, consensus agreement, etc.) and the types of mechanisms (working group, advisory group, evaluation team, etc.). It quickly became clear, however, that this resource was not going to work in this context. All decisions follow the same process of consulting with peers at the same level in the hierarchy, and then informing downward, as outlined above. The suggestion of including stakeholders across MOLISA (national), DOLISA (provincial), BOLISA (district), and commune levels in committees, for example, was completely counter to the organizational systems in place. Again, there was no scope for involving other stakeholders, especially those closer to the implementation, in decisions about the design, implementation, or use of the M&E. The options we had set out in our grid did not match any of the decision-making processes in place, and the concept of different decision-making groups just did not apply.

The second insight came from reflecting on the dynamics during the workshop, and, in particular, on expectations of expertise. Noske-Turner approached her role as that of a 'facilitator' of a participatory process, in which the decisions and plans would ultimately be made by the MOLISA participants, rather than as an 'expert'. However, particularly in the workshop focused on deciding on key M&E questions and matching those with methods, it became clear that this was causing tensions. The MOLISA participants seemed frustrated that Noske-Turner was not being directive enough. The process of discussing and prioritizing 'what do we need to know' was unfamiliar and inherently open-ended, especially compared with more linear processes such as results-based management. More significantly, they expected an expert who would seek their input but ultimately would provide a proposal about what to do. The messiness of the process, and lack of direct input by the 'expert', was quite alien and risked being perceived as incompetence, reflecting especially badly on the facilitator, who was expected to provide technical expertise, and also risking damage to the relationship with UNICEF. Expectations of expertise and the ways in which this can undermine participatory processes have been noted by others as a challenge in Vietnam and elsewhere in the region (Nicetic and van de Fliert, 2014). Our experience shows that, in Vietnam, efforts to use 'participatory' approaches, as understood in C4D and evaluation literature, can be uncomfortable and ineffective due to these differing expectations.

Rethinking how to foster participatory approaches in Vietnam

So far we have discussed how the bureaucratic structures of development, which tend to entrench top-down, pre-planned, and upward accountability, operate in tandem with the government of Vietnam's systems, which heavily rely on vertical, hierarchical processes. This means that commonly used participatory approaches from around the world are not just limited but usually not applicable. To make meaningful change in the systems towards accommodating participatory approaches, common strategies must be rethought and more direct engagement is needed with the government systems influencing practice. Specifically, a two-pronged approach is necessary: first, sustained advocacy to strengthen legal frameworks and implementation; and second, the promotion of sectoral and societal changes in the expectation of greater and more meaningful participation.

Advocacy work to influence laws and legal frameworks over recent years indicates what this means. UNICEF is one organization that is mandated with realizing children's rights, with the principal and cross-cutting right to participation having a bearing on all other rights. UNICEF Vietnam has advocated that listening to children acts as an antidote to making sweeping generalizations about them and their views in life (Woodhead, 1998). This has practical benefits for children and their communities, and through the evaluation of child rights implementation practices (Hart et al., 2004). UNICEF Vietnam, with other child rights-mandated partners, advocates for international norms and standards on child participation to be incorporated in overarching legal frameworks. The Law on Protection, Care, and Education of Children was first amended in 2004 with a focus on altering some articles. The second amendment, which began in 2013 and in which UNICEF Vietnam and other partners were extensively involved, was considered to be a comprehensive and significant amendment. It aimed to: 1) address the emerging vulnerability and uncertainty children are facing in Vietnam's fast-changing context; 2) better harmonize with international child rights standards; and 3) provide detailed guidance for implementing the constitution and other relevant legislation relating to children. The amended law was finally approved on 5 April 2016 by the National Assembly and took effect from June 2017.

The strategy involved gathering and providing evidence on child rights implementation, identifying existing legal gaps, using international best practice, and actively engaging with both the government's child law drafting team and the appraisal team in the National Assembly. Identification of key advocacy influencers among the decision makers and the National Assembly members was also a crucial step towards the goal. Social media platforms were used to generate public debates on issues concerning the child law. As a result of this prolonged advocacy process, a chapter on child participation in Vietnam was included in the revised 2017 Child Law.

To some extent, the success of this local advocacy in promoting participatory approaches through system strengthening has triggered further effects in policy development. For example, a government budget was allocated to the National Programme on Child Participation in order to meet the objectives by 2020. Notably, the programme spelled out a clear role for children and adolescents in monitoring and evaluating child rights implementation, including in evaluating communication. Furthermore, children's councils have been introduced as a model of participation across the country at the community level. This was crucial in preventing top-down and ineffective enforcement of the law and the national programme. The initiative, drawn from best practices of child participation in Latin America and in other countries in the region where children's and young people's representation is mandatory and legally binding in policymaking bodies, was replicated in 27 provinces across the country. It functions around the core principle of children influencing decisions in local decision-making processes on issues related to their lives. At the same time, it promotes communication, raises awareness on child rights, and generates attention and support from the community and the society in realizing child rights.

The second component of the two-pronged approach was community-based interventions, including behavioural and social change initiatives, to address traditional views of participation. In this work, mass media and social media played an influential role in amplifying changes and promoting children's and youth voices. Young people were encouraged to debate from a rights-based angle and to contribute to discussions on social issues and decision making. Specifically, instead of following the traditional approach of normative participation, in which academically gifted children are selected by adults in schools to represent their peers on platforms where children's and youth voices are solicited, members of the children's councils are volunteers, diverse, and nominated by the children themselves to represent them in different forums for youth. These forums include regular and periodic meetings with provincial and city leaders on social and economic development planning. In addition, to make youth voices heard at the central decision-making level, MOLISA organizes a national children's forum every two years that gathers children from all the provinces in the country for a week-long event, culminating in a presentation of their debates and dialogues to policymakers at the highest level. These are televised for the public and have the participation of development partners, and policymakers and leaders are bound to report back on progress on any plans committed to at the next forum to ensure accountability. Pertinent examples include a controversy over trees being cut down in Hanoi in 2015, and increased media coverage of cases of child and female sexual abuse.

In this way, it is important to embed participation in the evaluation of C4D initiatives in general, and child and citizen participation in particular. Given the hierarchical and vertical nature of government systems and broader cultural systems in Vietnam, enhancing opportunities for participation requires pushing for law and policy change and implementation as part of a locally tailored approach. It is a piece of the puzzle that, when put together, can gradually bring about a changed picture.

Conclusion

Our experiments to bring a greater level of participation into the evaluation of C4D in Vietnam floundered for a number of reasons. The collaboration began with high levels of enthusiasm to work with the Evaluating C4D framework among the UNICEF Vietnam teams involved, with a specific interest in involving children, parents, and guardians, and this flowed into the writing of the TOR. However, the consultant came from quite a different starting point and took a much more pragmatic approach. Some interactive methods were able to be used as an 'add-on' to the main methods, but it was difficult to use them to their full extent given their dependency on time for trust building and rapport. The workshops with government officials, intended to develop an M&E plan for a national communication programme, faced problems before they even started, with the schedule cut from three half-day sessions to just two meetings, approximately three hours in total. More than anything else, however, both these initiatives struggled because they used models of participation from elsewhere. Although the methods and processes work well and can be adapted to suit many situations, the meaning, approach to, and expectations of participation need to be rethought in the context in Vietnam since it is so different from, for example, Latin America, Africa, India, and other regions contributing significantly to scholarship on and the practice of participatory methodology.

Contrary to initial appearances, there is, in fact, currently much potential to use participatory processes in Vietnam. Perhaps counterintuitively, strategies that work with the vertical hierarchies of government and that use bureaucratic efficiency are more likely to succeed, compared with working against systems by trying to force them to be more horizontal and dialogical. This is evidenced in this chapter by outlining the use of policy advocacy strategies to mandate the right to participation, and the use of guidance to ensure that implementation is not tokenistic, coupled with social change efforts to normalize participation. Once such processes are mandated in legal frameworks, the government systems can effectively follow through, including by requiring participatory processes that involve children in the evaluation of communication programmes. These strategies for creating spaces for participation may not be immediately familiar to outsiders, and they may fall short of international ideals in some ways. On the other hand, the scale of participation and speed of change are remarkable. More importantly, the processes work because they are culturally and contextually appropriate.

Notes

1. <https://www.betterevaluation.org/en/evaluation-options/after_action_review> [accessed 24 November 2014].
2. <https://www.betterevaluation.org/sites/default/files/EA_PM%26E_toolkit_module_4_CLFS_for_publication.pdf> [accessed 24 November 2014].
3. <http://ear.findingavoice.org/intro/2-0.html> [accessed 24 November 2014].

References

Abuza, Z. (2015) *Stifling the Public Sphere: Media and Civil Society in Vietnam*, National Endowment for Democracy, Washington DC.

Armytage, L. (2011) 'Evaluating aid: an adolescent domain of practice', *Evaluation* 17 (3): 261–76 <https://doi.org/10.1177/1356389011410518>.

Chambers, R. (1983) *Rural Development: Putting the Last First*, Longman, Burnt Mill, Essex.

Chambers, R. (2012) *Revolutions in Development Inquiry*, Routledge, Abingdon.

Chouinard, J.A. (2013) 'The case for participatory evaluation in an era of accountability', *American Journal of Evaluation* 34 (2): 237–53 <https://doi.org/10.1177/1098214013478142>.

Cornwall, A. and Brock, K. (2005) 'What do buzzwords do for development policy? A critical look at "participation", "empowerment" and "poverty reduction"', *Third World Quarterly* 26 (7): 1043–60 <https://doi.org/10.1080/01436590500235603>.

Dutta, M.J. (2011) *Communicating Social Change: Structure, Culture, and Agency*, Routledge, New York and Abingdon.

Fitzpatrick, J.L., Sander, J.R. and Worthen, B.R. (2004) *Program Evaluation: Alternative Approaches and Practical Guidelines*, 3rd edn, Allyn and Bacon, Boston MA.

Fraser, C. and Restrepo-Estrada, S. (1998) *Communicating for Development: Human Change for Survival*, I.B. Tauris, London and New York.

Freire, P. (2000) *Pedagogy of the Oppressed*, 30th anniversary edn, Continuum, New York.

Hart, R. et al. (2004) *Stepping Back from 'The Ladder': Reflections on a Model of Participatory Work with Children*, Springer, Dordrecht.

Laverack, G. and Huy Dap, D. (2003) 'Transforming information, education and communication in Vietnam', *Health Education* 103 (6): 363–9.

Lennie, J. and Tacchi, J. (2013) *Evaluating Communication for Development: A Framework for Social Change*, Earthscan/Routledge, New York.

Manyozo, L. (2006) 'Manifesto for development communication: Nora Quebral and the Los Baños school of development communication', *Asian Journal of Communication* 16 (1): 79–99.

Manyozo, L. (2012) *Media, Communication and Development: Three Approaches*, Sage, London.

Manyozo, L. (2017) *Communicating Development with Communities*, Routledge, Abingdon.

McElwee, P.D. and Ha, H.L. (2006) *Deepening Democracy and Increasing Popular Participation in Viet Nam*, United Nations Development Programme, Hanoi.

Melkote, S.R. (2003) 'Theories of development communication', in B. Moody (ed.), *International and Development Communication: A 21st-Century Perspective*, pp. 129–46, Sage, London.

Minh, T.T., Larsen, C.E.S. and Neef, A. (2010) 'Challenges to institutionalizing participatory extension: the case of farmer livestock schools in Vietnam', *Journal of Agricultural Education and Extension* 16 (2): 179–94.

Morris, N. (2003) 'A comparative analysis of the diffusion and participatory models in development communication', *Communication Theory* 13 (2): 225–48 <https://doi.org/10.1111/j.1468-2885.2003.tb00290.x>.

Nicetic, O. and van de Fliert, E. (2014) 'Changing institutional culture: PM&E in transdisciplinary research for development', in *11th European IFSA Symposium, Berlin Germany*. Available from: <http://ifsa.boku.ac.at/cms/fileadmin/Proceeding2014/WS_1_7_Nicetic.pdf> [accessed 17 December 2019].

Noske-Turner, J. (2017) *Rethinking Media Development through Evaluation: Beyond Freedom*, Palgrave Macmillan/Springer, Cham, Switzerland.

Quaghebeur, K., Masschelein, J. and Nguyen, H.H. (2004) 'Paradox of participation: giving or taking part?', *Journal of Community and Applied Social Psychology* 14 (3): 154–65.

Quarry, W. and Ramírez, R. (2009) *Communication for Another Development: Listening before Telling*, Zed Books, London.

Quebral, N. (1976) *Development Communication*, Southeast Asian Centre for Graduate Study and Research in Agriculture, Laguna, Philippines.

Servaes, J. (2000) 'Reflections on the differences in Asian and European values and communication modes', *Asian Journal of Communication* 10 (2): 53–70.

Supadhiloke, B. (2013) 'Right to communicate, public participation, and democratic development in Thailand', in J. Servaes (ed.), *Sustainability Participation and Culture in Communication*, Intellect, Bristol and Chicago.

Thomas, P. and van de Fliert, E. (2014) *Interrogating the Theory and Practice of Communication for Social Change: The Basis for a Renewal*, Palgrave Macmillan, Basingstoke and New York.

Tufte, T. (2017) *Communication and Social Change: A Citizen Perspective*, John Wiley and Sons, Chichester.

Tung Hieu, L.Y. (2016) 'Confucian influences on Vietnamese culture', *Vietnam Social Sciences* 5: 71.

UNICEF Vietnam (2010) *UNICEF Policy Brief on Child Participation*, UNICEF Vietnam, Hanoi.

Waisbord, S. (2001) *Family Tree of Theories, Methodologies and Strategies in Development Communication*. Communication for Social Change. Available from: <http://www.communicationforsocialchange.org/pdf/familytree.pdf>.

Waisbord, S. (2008) 'The institutional challenges of participatory communication in international aid', *Social Identities* 14 (4): 505–22 <https://doi.
org/10.1080/13504630802212009>.

White, S. (1996) 'Depoliticizing development: the uses and abuses of participation', *Development in Practice* 6 (1): 142–55 <https://doi.org/10.1080/096
1452961000157564>.

Wilkins, K.G. (2018) 'Communication about development and the challenge
of doing well: donor branding in the West Bank', in F. Enghel and J. Noske-
Turner (eds), *Communication in International Development*, pp. 92–112,
Routledge, Abingdon.

Woodhead, M. (1998) *Children's Perspectives on their Working Lives*, Rädda
Barnen, Stockholm.

Author biographies

Tran Phuong-Anh is a communications specialist with experience in
communication for advocacy and communication for behaviour and social
change. She has been working for UNICEF since 2006 after a postgraduate
degree from the University of Leeds. Prior to UNICEF Vietnam, she was a
journalist.

Jessica Noske-Turner is a lecturer in Media and Creative Industries,
Loughborough University London. From 2014 to 2017 she was a postdoc-
toral fellow at RMIT University, contributing to the *Evaluating C4D: Supporting
Adaptive and Accountable Development* research project.

Ho Anh Tung is a graduate from the University of Birmingham with an interest
in ethnographic research. From 2015 to 2017 he was a research assistant on
the *Evaluating C4D: Supporting Adaptive and Accountable Development* research
project based at RMIT University Vietnam in Hanoi.

CHAPTER 4

Exploring sanitation: participatory research design and ethnography in West Bengal

Jo Tacchi, Tripta Chandola, Vinod Pavarala and Rania Elessawi

This chapter describes the use of a participatory and ethnographic approach to explore a sanitation campaign in the Nadia District of West Bengal. The research took place from late 2015 until mid-2016, around a year after Nadia District was proclaimed Open Defecation Free (ODF). Ethnographic approaches are most often considered in development work for situation analysis or formative research. In this case, however, we took this approach for a 'retrospective analysis' of the Sabar Souchagar *(Latrines for All) campaign (SSC) in Nadia District. The chapter explores the research design in relation to the participatory, complex, and critical components of the Evaluating Communication for Development (C4D) framework, and concludes with some observations about the applications of this approach in C4D research and evaluation.*

Keywords: Communication for Development; ethnography; participatory; sanitation

Introduction

This chapter describes the participatory and ethnographic approach used to explore a sanitation campaign in the Nadia District of West Bengal as part of the overall Evaluating Communication for Development (C4D) intervention. The research took place from late 2015 until mid-2016, around a year after Nadia District was proclaimed Open Defecation Free (ODF). Ethnographic approaches are most often considered in development work for situation analysis or formative research. Connecting ethnography with action research can provide a project development approach that has been applied during project implementation in a number of ICT and development projects (Tacchi, 2015). In this case, however, we took this approach for a 'retrospective analysis' of the *Sabar Souchagar* (Latrines for All) campaign (SSC) in Nadia District.

In this chapter we first explain the background to the research, the approach of SSC, and why an ethnographic approach was taken. We then go into the details of the research design and describe how this had two parts. The first part included a stakeholder analysis involving stakeholder

http://dx.doi.org/10.3362/9781780449968.004

mapping and preliminary research with stakeholders to get their inputs into the main research design. The second part took an ethnographic approach to understand elements of the complexity of SSC from a range of different perspectives. The chapter goes on to explore the research design in relation to the participatory, complex, and critical components of the Evaluating C4D framework (Lennie and Tacchi, 2013) through a discussion of some of the findings. We conclude the chapter with some observations about when and why this two-part approach may be usefully applied in C4D research and evaluation, when ethnography may be useful, and the kinds of skills and experience such an approach requires.

Background

The open defecation initiative in Nadia District, West Bengal achieved widespread recognition as a uniquely successful case. In 2015 it made a declaration of ODF status, meaning that all families and transient populations in the district now had access to and used toilets, something that has been an ongoing 'problem' in India for decades (Coffey and Spears, 2017; Gupta et al., 2014; Doron and Jeffrey, 2014; Patwa and Pandit, 2018). The sanitation programme that led to this declaration was conceptualized and overseen by Nadia's District Magistrate. A District Magistrate is the highest state-appointed official at the district level. Nadia has a population of 5.2 million.

The approach the District Magistrate took was heralded as successful and unique in the way in which it mobilized a range of stakeholder groups and comprehensively addressed both supply and demand issues. This meant growing the sanitation infrastructure through the manufacture of parts and the building of latrines as well as influencing sanitation practices and demand for toilets through communication and subsidized provision. It incorporated elements of a collective action approach, including engaging diverse stakeholders around an agreed common agenda, undertaking iterative planning and implementation, and ensuring effective dialogue and ongoing shared learning informed by evidence to bring about social change.

The District Magistrate launched the SSC in October 2013. The challenging target he set for the district was to provide a latrine for every single household and achieve 100 per cent ODF status within a year. According to the government's Swachh Bharat Mission baseline survey in 2012, the district had 30.67 per cent of households without a latrine.[1] ODF status was achieved within 18 months, six months longer than the target set originally by the District Magistrate. The delay was reported as being due to elections taking place during the first 12 months. It was recognized as a significant achievement, completed in a short time, when the West Bengal government declared Nadia as the country's *first* 100 per cent ODF district in April 2015, under the government's Swachh Bharat Mission programme.

In accounting for this unique success, it is important to recognize the broader character of the district, not least the fact that almost 70 per cent of the district already had latrines when the SSC was launched. In fact, Nadia is one of the most prosperous districts in West Bengal, with a textile- and agriculture-based economy. There is no scarcity of water: the district is served by four rivers and its name is literally translated as 'river'. Nadia also has a high literacy rate (75 per cent, according to the 2011 census). In addition, sanitation received particular and dedicated attention from the District Magistrate. For him, SSC was his 'signature' project, a special issue he wanted to address because it was an issue around which it would be easy to forge a consensus, and, as far as he could see, it was something that could be fixed within a limited time. As such, he felt that he could make a difference during his term as District Magistrate (terms are usually two years) and he was professionally committed to the SSC, using both his position of power and powers of persuasion for its success.

The SSC was highly visible in Nadia, with high investment in information, education, and communication (IEC) and the strong and charismatic leadership of the District Magistrate. There was a sense of urgency and momentum to achieve ODF that was linked on the one hand to shame and disease, and on the other to a sense of pride and a right to sanitation and improved health. The funding allocated for IEC was greater than for previous sanitation schemes in the district, leading to saturation and good-quality IEC materials, media coverage, and events. The District Magistrate managed IEC budgets from various other and related development schemes and combined new sanitation funding with existing and continuing funds from other government programmes to maximize the availability of resources for the SSC as a whole. The efforts were focused on social mobilization and community activities such as meetings organized through faith-based organizations and schools, and a mini marathon with banner slogans such as 'Nadia Run out of Shame 2015'. The District Magistrate was also able to mobilize private-sector companies, particularly by engaging the state chapter of the Confederation of Indian Industries to support the numerous district-wide campaign activities with financial and in-kind resources. The highly visible *Sabar Shouchagar* Express was a van that drove around the district attracting crowds; it had a wall for signatures (pledges to stop open defecation) on one side, and on the other a stage for folk musicians and speakers. Messages on the van included 'Our latrine our image'. A hot air balloon was utilized, with the message 'Latrine for all is our right', and the district claimed to have organized the longest human chain against open defecation, which attracted a lot of media coverage and was widely publicized. A sanitation pledge was made and reaffirmed weekly by all schoolchildren, there were street plays and rallies, posters, banners, leaflets, and short films, and a range of training and motivation sessions and meetings for various influencer and stakeholder groups.

UNICEF became aware of the SSC and its achievements in early 2015 as the district was approaching ODF status. By mid-2015, Nadia's SSC had been researched through surveys and narrative accounts, including a 'Rapid assessment' by the TARU Research and Information Network in August 2015 (TARU, 2015); *The Story of ODF Nadia*,[2] a film available through UNICEF's online repository of communication materials; and an earlier UNICEF and Hijli Inspiration report (2014) that assessed latrine use and behaviour change and undertook a situation analysis. Nevertheless, important questions remained unanswered. How was the SSC so successful in such a short space of time while other campaigns elsewhere in India had not been? What had been done differently here? Was the ODF status sustainable? Was it replicable?

Through discussions with C4D and Water, Sanitation, and Hygiene (WASH) teams in UNICEF India, we developed an approach designed to go beyond the survey data and narrative accounts, to understand why the SSC was so successful in eradicating open defecation in such a short time frame, to identify possible issues for sustainability, and to understand if the approach was replicable. Questions about sustainability and replicability were being asked with some urgency. What are the factors that pose challenges to sustainability, including infrastructural, social, cultural, historical, political, and other factors? Is the approach undertaken in Nadia replicable in other contexts? Given the complexity of the questions and the importance of considering them within the local context, it was agreed that an ethnographic approach was most likely to provide the kind of rich insights required to complement existing survey data and findings.

Ethnography is an iterative approach based on the idea of generating rich description through direct and sustained interaction with people in their everyday lives. Key methods include participant observation, in-depth interviews, and various techniques aimed at understanding people's perspectives, practices, meanings, and experiences (Hammersley and Atkinson, 2007). If time and resources allow, ethnography can provide valuable insights into complex situations and help identify the range of opportunities and constraints available to different sections of society. Before beginning the ethnographic part of the research, however, we needed to undertake a stakeholder analysis, to get a sense of the context and range of perspectives and to find out from those involved at all levels of the SSC where they felt we should focus our questions and effort.

Research design

The first thing we did to gain a preliminary understanding of the SSC was to visit Nadia, undertake a stakeholder analysis, and engage with a range of people from key stakeholder groups. This was intended to capture a range of perspectives and experiences, to begin to identify the theories of change among these groups, and to engage them in the framing and design of the second, ethnographic part of the study. Did they consider the SSC to have been a success? What made it so? What were the issues that might threaten the sustainability of ODF in the future? How could our research help? Who did they think we should talk to?

We undertook 20 individual and group interviews with 11 stakeholder groups, using semi-structured sets of questions and themed and exploratory discussions. The interviews highlighted a range of concerns, particularly around sustainability, such as the lack of funding for the maintenance of latrines and the continued practice of latrine use. These concerns about sustainability, from administrative-level respondents in particular, focused on marginal population groups and we were urged by stakeholders to ensure that our research engaged with these people.

With insights gained from the discussions and interviews with stakeholders, the research design was developed with the following objectives:

1. to deepen understanding of the **process** followed in Nadia and how high levels of engagement and **mobilization** were achieved, as well as the role of **communication** in this;
2. to understand **contextual** factors and how these relate to both the success and **sustainability** of the SSC;
3. through the research findings, to evaluate how the SSC's success in Nadia has **replicability** for application in other contexts.

Each objective was developed into research questions and protocols to form an overarching research design (see Figure 4.1), informed by stakeholder analysis and engagement. It was clear from our first discussions with stakeholders that the SSC followed a highly adaptive and effective process (objective 1). The District Magistrate told us that he followed a target-orientated, deadline approach, adapting activities and plans along the way to achieve the end goal. For him, a clear 'strategy' emerged only at the end, but he recognized the effectiveness of engaging all aspects of government and administration from district to local level, utilizing networks of front-line workers at the community level, and engaging in highly effective IEC. To understand how mobilization occurred, we developed three key research questions from which we developed more detailed interview protocols. The interviews were designed to help us map the various aspects and experiences of mobilization at all levels from government to citizen, including bureaucratic mobilization as well as community mobilization. This covered people's ideas about influence, their theories of change, and how information and communication had flowed and been experienced.

We knew from our initial research with stakeholders that issues of sustainability were both complex and contextual (objective 2). We needed to include the perspectives of a range of people to develop a nuanced understanding of the sustainability factors that were significant for the SSC, including social (community participation), individual (behavioural change), and infrastructural (maintenance, repair, and construction of latrines). Preliminary research had also alerted us to the complex relationship between supply and demand, including the tapestry of social, cultural, financial, and infrastructural considerations that informed demand.

Objective 3 was about replicability. The research questions here focused on principles and practices that may point to ways in which the success

Research design

Mapping mobilization
- Map mobilization and spheres of influence
- Chart the various theories of change
- Communicative ecologies

Critique of complexity
- Contextual factors
- Sustainability factors
- Supply and demand

Principles and practices
- Identification of guiding principles in practice
- Overarching theory of change and SiEQ
- Core mobilization actions

Blueprint for spreadability

Sabar souchagar

Retrospective analysis

Key research questions

Adaptive process
- How was the level of mobilization achieved?
- What were the key influence points and processes?
- How was communication effectively used?

Context & sustainability
- What are the particularities of Nadia?
- What are the key sustainability factors?
- How might we conceptualize supply and demand?

Spreadability
- What were the key principles behind the campaign?
- What were the key practices leading to success?
- How far are these replicable in other locations?

Scoping visit & inclusive research design

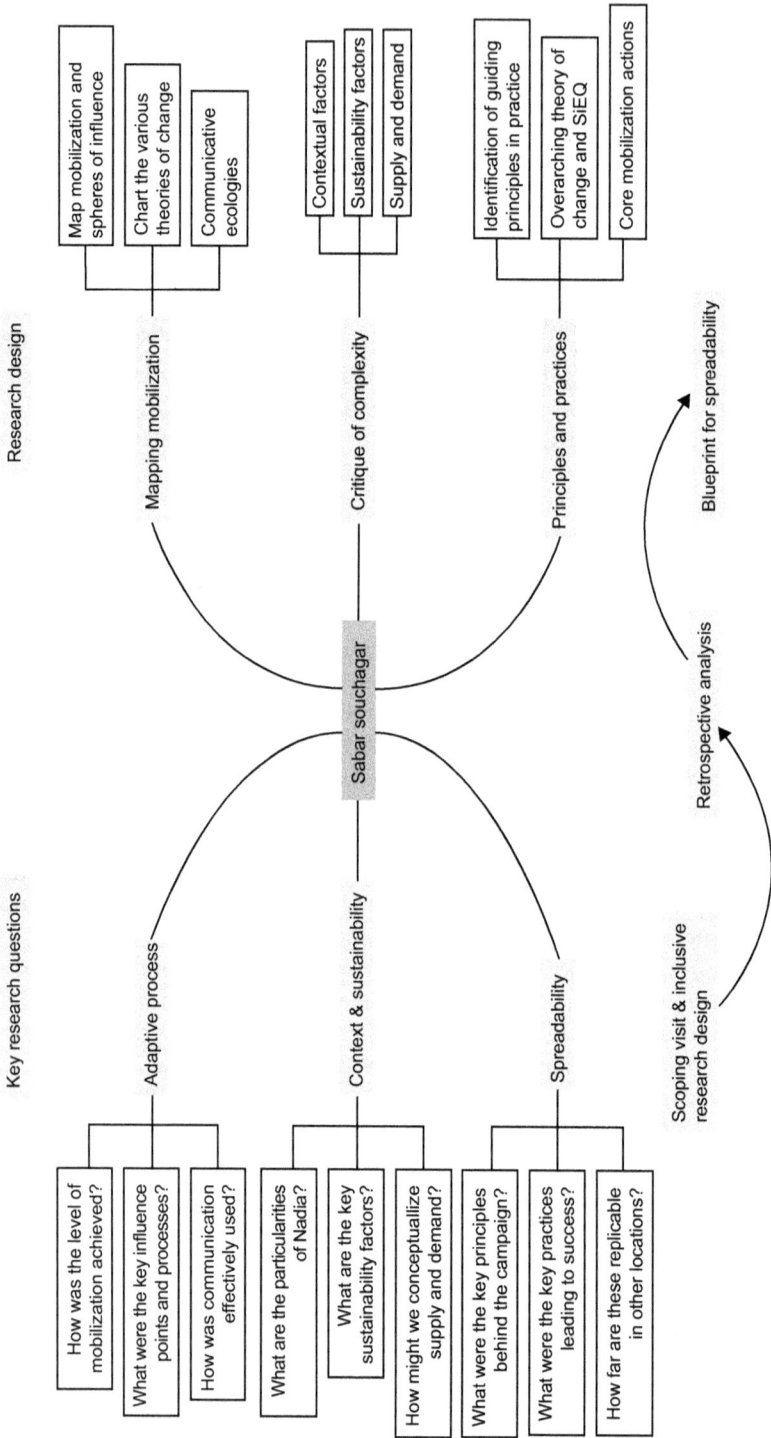

Figure 4.1 Visualization of the research design

of the SSC might be repeated elsewhere (we used the term 'spread-ability' in our research design). We knew from our initial visit to Nadia and discussions with the District Magistrate and other senior officials that straightforward replication was unlikely, for example because of the particular characteristics of Nadia and the District Magistrate's determined focus on and commitment to the success of the SSC. Understanding the underlying principles, such as the adaptive approach taken by the District Magistrate, can provide a guide or framework that can be applied in other contexts, since it does not predetermine specific actions or depend on specific contextual factors, but on driving principles and goals. Examples of practice can help inform the means to achieve the goals and can be adapted to suit different situations.

In the ethnographic part of the research, we conducted research across urban and rural areas in the district. These included slums, villages, brick kilns, schools, and district administration offices, among others. We conducted 40 interviews, with both individuals and groups, during three field visits. We used a local research assistant as a guide and translator during the field visits and liaised with and received support from the UNICEF West Bengal Office. Transcriptions of interviews and fieldnotes were coded and analysed using qualitative analysis software.

Implications of the approach: links to the framework

In this section of the chapter we describe the research design in terms of three components from the Evaluating C4D framework: participatory, complex, and critical. We do this by drawing on some of our research findings to illustrate the importance of these components to a study of this kind.

Participatory

We took a participatory research design approach in the first stage. This involved engaging with a range of stakeholders. UNICEF provided us with a list of the range of key stakeholders thought to have played a role in the success of the SSC. We added to the list after our initial stakeholder engagements, and during the second part of the research we grouped these stakeholders into six categories:

1. administrative (state, district, block, *gram panchayat*, municipality);
2. elected members (district, block, village);
3. front-line workers (Anganwadi, accredited social health activist);
4. rural sanitary marts (RSMs);
5. education, faith, and cultural institutions;
6. community (households, self-help groups, Nazardari committees).

We developed understanding of the main theories of change across these different stakeholder groups, as broadly summarized in Table 4.1.

Table 4.1 Theories of change across stakeholder groups

Stakeholder group	Theory of change	Key themes
Administrators (state, district, block, *gram panchayat*, municipality)	According to this group, the things that led to ODF status are: • operational and functional, sequenced mobilization • efficient governance and use of resources • careful planning and conceptualization, with the agility to change • access to sanitary toilets along with behaviour change communications • building on earlier initiatives • infrastructure capacities (subsidized) that enhance the possibility (and desire) for behavioural change.	Planning Management Demand generation Behaviour change
Elected members (district, block, village)	Elected members thought that their endorsement of the SSC and their active involvement in different awareness campaigns made the people in their respective constituencies confident about their own participation in the campaign.	Influencer engagement Endorsement led to trust Advocacy
Front-line workers (Anganwadi, accredited social health activist)	Raising awareness of available schemes and understanding and choosing healthier lifestyles leads to long-term behavioural change. Coordinating and ensuring that the communication about ODF and its benefits was understood by all the different front-line workers. The value of information dissemination networks at localized levels.	Awareness raising Behavioural change Local networks
Rural sanitary marts	The community mobilization, demand generation, and awareness campaigns undertaken during the SSC, along with funding and effective delivery mechanisms of better-quality and economically viable latrines led to ODF.	Mobilization (demand) Adequate funding and quality products (supply)
Education, faith, and cultural institutions	Education: Social motivation and peer pressure led to sustained behaviour change. Faith: Spreading messages about healthy and clean lifestyles and social practices led to motivated communities.	Mobilization Behaviour change Community monitoring Awareness raising Mobilization
Community[3]	Community-level Nazardari committees: Peer pressure and shaming eliminate open defecation. Marginal communities: Access to and awareness of schemes and subsidies and quality latrines led to the take-up of provision.	Community monitoring and surveillance Equity focus Access Funding

An examination of the theories of change across these stakeholder groups, and the differences between and in some cases within them, was instructive for our study. It helped us to understand the ways in which the SSC was experienced differently across and within stakeholder groups, as well as providing insights into a range of motivations for engaging with the SSC. It helped us determine the importance of 'mobilization' not just at the community level.

Indeed, key to the success of the SSC was the level of *bureaucratic* mobilization achieved, one that reached from district level all the way down to communities. What had happened in Nadia had been talked about as a 'social movement' because of the way it appeared to generate community mobilization. While the level of engagement across the district was indeed impressive, it was this effective *bureaucratic* mobilization that was particularly striking once we started to talk to people from across all the stakeholder groupings.

By including research respondents from across all of the stakeholder groups, we were able to construct our findings based on a multi-perspective understanding of the SSC. Our research showed that strong leadership from the highest official in the district led to a very effective and highly monitored pulling together of schemes and funding, including regular reporting at all levels of governance. The amount of monitoring of the SSC across all administrative levels, and at community level (which might be considered 'surveillance' by some), was matched by awareness raising. This was accompanied, where deemed necessary, by shaming and other punitive measures at the community level, monitored and/or administered by front-line workers and education and faith-based organizations as well as community-based committees. Overall, the SSC consisted of very focused communications with attention to a clearly defined goal and a timeline for reaching it. Thus, it was about effective bureaucratic mobilization combined with and contributing to community mobilization.

Overall strong and effective communications and strong messaging and oversight helped at all levels, from bureaucratic to community. However, when engaging with a range of perspectives, simplistic explanations or single perspective theories of change must be interrogated. From the perspective of marginalized groups – those widely identified as most at risk of threatening the sustainability of the SSC – we learned about some of the barriers facing them, including the issue of lack of funding for ongoing latrine maintenance. We learned that a simple behaviour change approach misses the fact that in many cases demand was already there; it was the *access to funding* and *provision of quality latrines* that prevented earlier take-up according to those we talked to.

A baseline survey was completed by the District Magistrate before the SSC began, and 'target' households were thus identified. Under the scrutiny and personal leadership of the District Magistrate, close attention to the end goal was maintained and an effective reporting mechanism was set up within administrative units at all jurisdictional levels. They were tasked with meeting the demands of the campaign – and were expected to do so – and were responsible for reporting on and monitoring systems to ensure time-bound delivery of the latrines. At the community level, through the surveillance and monitoring work of front-line workers, instances of open defecation were reduced. The close monitoring, ultimately overseen by the District Magistrate, led to a level of transparency throughout the layers of administration that also mitigated against improper use of funds or loss of focus on the end goal, according to our interviews with administrative officers. Checks and balances applied to the governance of the SSC enabled it to address the needs (and bottlenecks) of communities. Well-defined orders, along with monitoring and evaluation via weekly reports from offices at all levels of governance, were reviewed at the district level. This is an example of what Akhil Gupta (2012) might characterize as a move from the more common bureaucratic production of arbitrariness within Indian administration to the bureaucratic production of effectiveness.

A participatory approach to our research, initially through the stakeholder analysis and stakeholder engagement to develop the research design, was important given the complexity of the subject of study and the need to engage with a range of groups, including the most marginalized – which is something all stakeholder groups urged us to do. It allowed us to be as inclusive as possible with a diversity of social groups, and to include a range of voices and experiences. A participatory approach to the research design meant respecting, legitimizing, and drawing on the knowledge and experience of all stakeholders, including community members. This meant that simple and uncontested views of how and why the SSC was successful were critiqued and questioned as overly simplistic. It allowed us to include a range of experiences and views to paint a more complex and critical picture, as will be shown below.

Complex

Open defecation is not a simple problem that can be solved with a simple approach, as illustrated by the vast literature on ODF initiatives across the world (e.g. Barnard et al., 2013; Mozaffar, 2014), in which it is recognized that the supply of latrines does not necessarily lead to use. Complex factors including marginalization, caste, class, and poverty have a central bearing on this. In the Indian context, where caste and gender play a crucial role in the structural, systemic, and everyday marginalization that these groups encounter, the matter of sanitation cannot be resolved solely on the premise of ensuring access to infrastructural amenities, particularly since the upkeep of these falls on these constituent groups (Desai et al., 2015; O'Reilly, 2018). The determination of the District Magistrate to achieve ODF status and the adaptive processes he set up and monitored to achieve this led to a necessarily flexible and problem-solving approach that aided identification of the barriers faced by the most marginalized and ways around them.

The initial focus of the SSC was on demand generation. While characterized in accounts of the SSC as a 'demand-generation phase', our research with a range of community members, including some of the most marginalized, suggests that it is more appropriate to consider this as an 'awareness-raising phase' – awareness, that is, of the subsidies available. Our discussions with people from a lower-caste weaver village reinforced the point that awareness of the funding available led to the uptake of latrines, that there was no resistance once it was understood that the funds were available. There was no apparent lack of demand for latrines among the less well-off; the key issue was awareness of the subsidies available, and then effectively drawing on funding schemes to provide good-quality latrines. This latter step is often a stumbling block, but in Nadia efficient and effective processes and structures were established to enable access to information about subsidies, support from front-line workers to obtain the subsidies, and then the actual provision of latrines, which was equally well structured.

The supply structures included RSMs and production centres, which were effectively supported and expanded through funding generated by the convergence of various schemes. The SSC created a subsidy-driven demand for latrines that the expanded network of RSMs met. At the same time, this relates to and highlights a serious sustainability issue linked to maintenance and funding. Our research suggests that the most vulnerable households are liable to return to open defecation if their latrines are damaged and in need of repair, or if they are not able to maintain them. The announcement of ODF status meant an end to most of the funding streams, and there was no provision within the SSC for maintenance. Maintenance is considered to be the responsibility of the latrine owner, and for those in the poorest sections of society, this shifts the onus onto poor people. With no provision of funding for maintenance, the sustainability of RSMs in the district is also a concern, likely to adversely affect the containment of open defecation once the latrines cannot be maintained by the poorer families.

Another issue uncovered by our research was the lack of attention to upgrading existing and unsanitary latrines. For example, in a lower-caste village, a group of women raised concerns about their households not being included in the initial beneficiary list drawn up during the SSC surveys undertaken in the district. Their households had not received any subsidy under any prior schemes and they were currently compelled to defecate in the open because of the insanitary state of their privately constructed latrines. Until the SSC, and the increased awareness of the subsidies available to them, they had not considered approaching the authorities. While the campaign was ongoing, highlighting the issue and the scheme, they approached the local GP office to ask why they were not included in the beneficiary list. They were informed that it was because they already had latrines on their premises.

These latrines had been constructed by the households at their own expense (2,000–3,000 rupees), with only a squatting plate, low-depth pit, and temporary materials such as plastic or cloth used as surrounding cover.

The women's awareness of the unhygienic impact of their insanitary latrines on their everyday lives was further consolidated by the intensive awareness campaigns and mobilization undertaken during the SSC. They were left with the unpleasant choice of using unsanitary and unhygienic latrines, or open defecation.

Our research also uncovered a level of concern about the sustainability of ODF status due to those households who had been beneficiaries of earlier sanitation schemes and subsidies, going back as far as 20 years, but who had since then received no maintenance subsidy. The research highlighted the concern that, while these households had a latrine, in many instances these were insanitary and essentially non-functional. For those with latrines supplied through the SSC too, the issue of maintenance in the future was raised regularly.

What the SSC did not address directly were larger (infra)structural inadequacies, such as sewage systems and waste disposal, the lack of which, our research shows, pose sustainability issues for ODF status in the future. Much of the population most vulnerable to a return to open defecation practices does not have running water or other sanitation-related services, such as sewage and waste disposal. Considering the SSC within a larger *sanitation ecology* can help understand how the creation of demand and the effective supply of latrines can fit into a broader and more structurally sustainable system, in which maintenance must be a feature. The strong results-based and narrow focus on the SSC led to success within a short time frame but there is now an urgent need to address funding for maintenance and to develop a broader sanitation ecology focus.

Another sustainability issue connected to funding relates to the effective mobilization of Anganwadi workers, who were identified as the key motivators at the community level. Anganwadi centres were set up to mobilize community members, with each Anganwadi centre covering 200 families and each centre consisting of a team of two workers. These workers were local women with an intimate knowledge of the area and its issues, and with a connection to the residents. During the intensive mobilization phase, the Anganwadi workers received incentives (30 rupees) for each eligible household they recruited into or validated for the SSC. They worked closely with RSMs, as only after the validation by an Anganwadi worker were the funds released for the latrines, from which both RSMs and Anganwadi workers drew their incentives. We found instances where these front-line workers significantly minimized their involvement in the campaign after the ODF declaration and the end of funding; this was understandable since they had been working on a commission basis.

Our approach to this research was deliberately complexity-based and designed to understand the many ways in which changes occurred in Nadia in response to the SSC. The details of the research above represent just a small part of our findings, but already they show that social and behaviour change is complex and involves processes and experiences that are often contradictory and continue to change after an initiative ends. It also shows that the SSC involved people and organizations with multiple perspectives and agendas, in an equally complex and adaptive approach utilizing a range of organizations and groups, networks and communities, incentives and punitive measures. Simple solutions to complex problems are unlikely, on their own, to achieve lasting success, while focusing on broader sanitation ecologies (in which open defecation is just one part) offers some interesting possibilities.

Critical

The critical component of the Evaluating C4D framework requires actively and explicitly addressing issues of difference – of gender, caste, ethnicity, age, economic situation, and any other relevant differences as well as unequal levels of access, power, and voice among participants. As advised by our stakeholders, we conducted fieldwork in locations that allowed us to engage with communities and stakeholders across diverse caste, communal, ethnic, and regional affiliations. For example, we deliberately conducted fieldwork in the only subdivision in the district to include 'notified areas' where slum settlements were identified. As our initial discussions with stakeholders suggested, we ensured that we talked to respondents from poor, marginalized, migrant, and mobile sections of the urban population, where issues of sustainability were felt to be most acute.

The vast literature on sanitation shows that subsidy by governments does not necessarily lead to adoption and use, even of affordable latrines, especially when marginalized and very poor people consider the ongoing costs of maintenance, which are not subsidized. Beliefs, values, and norms about purity and pollution influence the social acceptability of open defecation. Other research has found that people were discouraged from utilizing the affordable and government-subsidized pit latrines because they required manual pit emptying and this is a form of labour associated with scavenging and untouchability, and so people would prefer to use more expensive latrines that do not require manual pit emptying, or otherwise prefer to practise open defecation (Gupta et al., 2014). In the urban scenario, caste and communal affiliations play an important role in access and uptake of public latrines (Desai et al., 2015). In many cases, along with caste, socio-economic factors also affect access to sanitation (Mozaffar, 2014). The ecology of sanitation unfolds within particular social, cultural, and political systems.

While the most marginalized groups (for example, by caste or religion, migrant workers, slum dwellers, and people living below the poverty line) were seen as the primary target of the SSC, as they disproportionately represented those without latrines, they are also those with whom longer-term and more nuanced engagement is required that takes account of difference and prevalent inequalities. Inequalities are 'multi-dimensional, multi-layered and cumulative', and addressing them is central to achieving social justice (UNESCO, 2016). The use of 'pressure tactics' during the campaign will also have disproportionately singled out these groups, with consequences that are not fully known. Pressure tactics, where community members were issued with threats of social boycott, ration cards not being issued, and licences cancelled (in the case of brick kilns, which employ migrant labour), however effective they were or are thought to be, need to be closely scrutinized lest they reinforce existing inequalities and hierarchies.

While the result-driven campaign successfully mobilized the population and achieved ODF in a short time, for sustainability there needs to be attention to longer-term, deeper engagement with and understanding of the different groups and their dynamics, especially groups subject to persistent inequalities. Effective bureaucratic mobilization was realized by mapping the population in the district that had not benefited from sanitation subsidies, working towards a clear ODF goal; along the way, this meant identifying and addressing persistent challenges and barriers to the uptake of sanitation services (despite subsidized toilets), tapping into and raising demand and awareness in the identified sections of the population, and meeting these demands by effective delivery and construction mechanisms.

While we found that there was little or no resistance to subsidized and effective provision among the poorest and most marginalized groups, the discourse of others about these groups and their situations was remarkably dismissive. Some people's focus on behaviour change among the poorest misses the really different feature of the SSC: the change in behaviour of the bureaucrats and elites who in effect made the system work for the most marginalized. Despite this, there is still a perception that communities had to be mobilized in such an organized and effective manner to institute fundamental shifts in people's practice of defecating in the open on account of 'habituated' practices associated with 'traditional' social norms. One of the often-remarked refrains about the need for concentrated and consolidated behaviour change strategies was to disrupt the 'normalization' of open defecation as a practice. According to this narrative, the intensity of the campaign was needed for this reason, but also, in the view of some, because it was felt that 'the latrines are not important for the poor. They will not think twice about spending money on colour televisions, mobile phones, but latrines are not a priority for them' (block-level senior administrator). This is not what our research revealed.

In this and similar narratives, it was emphasized that the poor and illiterate need to be educated about the immediate and long-term benefits of having and using a latrine for their overall growth and development. Furthermore, the absence of latrines among these households was recognized as testimony to their resistance to the idea of development, and, according to a particular moral framework, to basic sanitation – conventionally considered as the state's responsibility – which is represented here as a consumer option or choice that loses out because the poor spend their money on televisions and mobile phones. This is part of a larger shifting imagination in which the poor might be seen as proactive, engaged consumers with the agency to exercise choice, and in such a view that choice is questioned with moralistic undertones

(Tacchi and Chandola, 2016). This leaves a question about the state's responsibilities towards disenfranchised citizens and their rights, subsidies, and entitlements. The example above collapses the discourse of 'cleanliness' and 'consumption' that emphasizes a loss of citizenship rights and the rise of the privileges and responsibilities of consumers (Chandola, 2013). What our research showed us was not a need for behaviour change per se but supported access to subsidized and accessible schemes, as well as community trust and confidence building in public-sector services.

The habit of open defecation was most commonly raised in our research in regard to structural inadequacies, social compulsions, poverty levels, and lack of awareness of the different schemes, as mentioned above. Yet we found that the groups who were the most 'resistant' and difficult to motivate in fact belonged to the landowning, prosperous Yadav and Ghosh communities. In some reported cases they were resistant to the idea of constructing latrines since they owned the land they defecated on and did not recognize open defecation as an issue for them – they could do what they wished on their own land. Among the poor, lower-caste, marginalized sections in the district, the instances of members defecating in the open were more complex as they did not own any land and would face social wrath if they used land owned by others or common land. This sometimes led to some households making do with unsanitary, unhygienic latrines, as detailed above.

To be clear, and to counter the strongly pejorative narratives offered by some respondents, our research highlighted not only that the poor, marginalized, and illiterate sections of communities were acutely aware of the role of latrines in ensuring their sustained hygienic well-being, but also that there was a strong demand from them. The main hurdles were finance and access constraints. Moreover, having a latrine and not being compelled to defecate in the open was seen and identified by community respondents as an 'aspirational' achievement and a marker of upward mobility in society.

The SSC caught the imagination of the population of Nadia though a very effective and intensive IEC campaign. The campaign activities engaged different groups, including women, children, and religious leaders. The activities were supported and attended by senior administrators and elected officials. Messages stressed shame in open defecation and pride in ODF status, safety of women and girls (mothers and sisters), and the right to a latrine and a clean environment. There was information on using and cleaning latrines, and having a latrine was linked to a happy family and the protection of children from diseases. The adaptive process and effective bureaucratic systems of provision, outreach, and monitoring led to an originally unintended but particularly effective level of trust and strengthened accountability for previously unserved and marginalized groups. This in turn made what was happening appear to some outsiders to be a social movement.

Our research shows two things worth noting here. First, poor communities (such as low-caste and tribal people, slum dwellers, and other people living below the poverty line) who were without latrines at the start of the SSC were already receptive to owning and using latrines; the major reason for not doing so was the cost. Therefore, the most useful awareness-raising parts of the SSC for them were those that informed them of their ability to access the scheme and its subsidies. Second, and related, the elements of communication that were among the most effective for these groups were the most local, face-to-face, and personal interactions with front-line workers and others engaged in mobilization at the community and household level, as here it became clear that subsidies were available and households were assisted in accessing them. This also facilitated a level of community dialogue, helping to identify barriers; given the strong monitoring and accountability features of the operationalization of the SSC, this also fed into adaptable processes.

Many of the sustainability concerns can be understood to relate to the continued 'infrastructural marginalization' of the excluded, for example through the lack of continuing support for maintaining and upgrading latrines. This must be approached critically, and data around this must be disaggregated by gender, caste, educational levels, and other relevant differences. Understandings growing from such data need to be considered in context-specific and culturally appropriate and sensitive ways. The persistent lack of 'social data' that are collected, analysed, reported, and tracked by government platforms perpetuates the lack of understanding of driving social development goals. Demand-generation strategies need to be conceptualized from an institutional and system perspective as much as the infrastructure objectives. Local social norms and the challenges, contradictions, and paradoxes that often characterize the process of social change need to be critically assessed, and evaluation carried out based on an awareness of the strengths and limitations of various evaluation approaches, methodologies, and methods, including participatory approaches. Being open to negative findings and learning from 'failure' are also important.

Applications of this approach

We conclude the chapter by considering when the two-part approach we employed may be usefully applied in C4D research and evaluation, either together or separately. Use of these approaches will, of course, depend on the research or evaluation questions you are seeking to answer.

Participatory research design

First is the participatory design part, including stakeholder mapping and engagement. This approach is really helpful for ensuring that the research or evaluation you are undertaking is both informed by and relevant to stakeholders. How you define the stakeholders is important, and in the Nadia SSC research we tried to be as inclusive as possible. The original list of stakeholders suggested to the research team did not include community members. Our discussions with those stakeholders listed – including administrators, elected representatives, RSMs, front-line workers, educators, and faith-based organizations – clearly indicated that it was essential for us to involve community members as a stakeholder group, and to engage with them in the ethnographic research phase.

This part of our research included this stakeholder mapping and engagement with each stakeholder group through a scoping visit. During that visit we talked to a range of people from across the stakeholder groups, to ask them about who else they felt we should talk to and what topics they felt were important in relation to issues such as sustainability – in other words, to help us with our research design. We also used our conversations to start to understand their theories of change. Getting a sense of the different positionings and perspectives of a range of stakeholders is really helpful in research design. It is an approach that ensures you are at least aware of the different perspectives and experiences, even if you end up focusing narrowly on specific issues, or on particular groups.

Ethnography

The C4D framework promotes the value of ongoing learning and continuous listening to a broad diversity of participants and stakeholders, and ethnography can be a useful approach for this. Ethnography is a research approach that demands a level of immersion in the field of research. As can be seen from the above, our ethnographic approach meant engaging, in situ, with a range of participants in an attempt to understand different experiences and perspectives. It is suitable to gaining insights into, and understandings of, situations of complexity, and/or to investigate complex issues, problems, or interventions.

It is well known that breakthrough initiatives and programmes that achieve high levels of success in one situation are rarely simply transferable to another. Contextual factors are central to understanding successes and planning future initiatives. Context factors include the whole range from the smallest-scale details such as local community relationships, histories, and customs to larger-scale structures and systems such as gender, caste, geography, economics, and politics, which themselves have histories and can be experienced differently by different social groupings. Often, the temptation is to try to boil down research and evaluation of situations and interventions into simple aspects or steps that can be followed and monitored. An ethnographic approach embraces complexity and multiple perspectives.

In this way, as we have discussed above, an ethnographic approach, while time-consuming, can provide insights into how and why a particular initiative works or does not work in a particular setting. It can also develop insights into the elements of success – especially process ones – that seem important considerations for replicability in other contexts. It can also inform programme design and programme adjustments, especially when it is linked with action research and embedded within organizations involved in an initiative (Tacchi, 2015).

Notes

1. <https://sbm.gov.in/sbmreport/Report/Physical/SBM_TargetVs AchievementWithout1314.aspx> [accessed 24 November 2019].
2. <http://www.unicefiec.org/document/the-story-of-odf-nadia-west-bengal> [accessed 24 November 2019].
3. In our ethnographic research, following inputs from initial research, we focused on groups such as slum dwellers, low-caste villages, migrant workers, self-help groups that were also RSMs, and Nazardari committee members.

References

Barnard, S., Routray, P., Majorin, F., Peletz, R., Boisson, S., Sinha, A. and Clasen, T. (2013) 'Impact of Indian Total Sanitation Campaign on latrine coverage and use: a cross-sectional study in Orissa three years following programme implementation', *PloS One* 8 (8): e71438.

Chandola, T. (2013) 'Dumped through technology: a policymaker's guide to disenfranchising slum dwellers', *Journal of Creative Communications* 8 (2–3): 265–75.

Coffey, D. and Spears, D. (2017) *Where India Goes: Abandoned Toilets, Stunted Development and the Costs of Caste*, HarperCollins, Noida, India.

Desai, R., McFarlane, C. and Graham, S. (2015) 'The politics of open defecation: informality, body, and infrastructure in Mumbai', *Antipode* 47 (1): 98–120.

Doron, A. and Jeffrey, R. (2014) 'Open defecation in India', *Economic and Political Weekly* 49 (49): 72–8.

Gupta, A. (2012) *Red Tape: Bureaucracy, Structural Violence, and Poverty in India*, Duke University Press, London.

Gupta, A., Spears, D., Coffey, D., Khurana, N., Srivastav, N., Hathi, P. and Vyas, S. (2014) 'Revealed preference for open defecation: evidence from a new survey in rural north India', *Economic and Political Weekly* 49 (38): 43–55.

Hammersley, M. and Atkinson, P. (2007) *Ethnography: Principles in Practice*, Routledge, Abingdon.

Lennie, J. and Tacchi, J. (2013) *Evaluating Communication for Development: A Framework for Social Change*, Earthscan/Routledge, New York.

Mozaffar, P. (2014) 'Open defecation and the human waste crisis in India', thesis, University of Kansas.

O'Reilly, K. (2018) 'The influence of land use changes on open defecation in rural India', *Applied Geography* 99: 133–9.

Patwa, J. and Pandit, N. (2018) 'Open defecation-free India by 2019: how villages are progressing?', *Indian Journal of Community Medicine* 43 (3): 246–7.

Tacchi, J. (2015) 'Ethnographic action research: media, information and communicative ecologies for development initiatives', in H. Bradbury (ed.), *The SAGE Handbook of Action Research*, Sage, London.

Tacchi, J. and Chandola, T. (2016) 'Complicating connectivity: women's negotiations with smartphones in an Indian slum', in L. Hjorth and O. Khoo (eds), *Routledge Handbook of New Media in Asia*, Routledge, Oxford.

TARU (2015) 'Rapid assessment of validation of sanitation coverage and use in Nadia District', unpublished report submitted to UNICEF.

UNESCO (2016) *World Social Science Report, 2016. Challenging Inequalities: Pathways to a Just World*, UNESCO, Paris. Available from: <https://en.unesco.org/wssr2016> [accessed 24 November 2019].

UNICEF and Hijli Inspiration (2014) '*Sabar Shouchagar*: an emerging and inspiring model', unpublished report.

Author biographies

Jo Tacchi is a professor and the Associate Dean of Research at Loughborough University London. She was the Chief Investigator on the *Evaluating C4D: Supporting Adaptive and Accountable Development* research project.

Tripta Chandola is an ethnographer and independent researcher based in Delhi, India. She has held research positions at NUS, Singapore and RMIT, Melbourne, and has also worked as a research consultant for several international and national projects. She led the ethnographic fieldwork for the retrospective analysis of the *Sabar Souchagar* campaign.

Vinod Pavarala is a professor in the Department of Communication at the University of Hyderabad, and holds the UNESCO Chair for Community Media. He was a Partner Investigator on the *Evaluating C4D: Supporting Adaptive and Accountable Development* research project.

Rania Elessawi is currently a Communication for Development Specialist, Programme Division, based in UNICEF's New York headquarters. Previously she was a C4D specialist at the UNICEF India Country Office, based in New Delhi.

CHAPTER 5

Using 'tepetepe' for understanding the complexity of people's lives in Malawi

Julie Elliott, Madalo Esther Samati,
Jessica Noske-Turner and Patricia Rogers

Traditional ways of doing monitoring and evaluation (M&E) can be poorly suited to the complex nature of Communication for Development (C4D) because of their assumptions of predictable and linear processes of planning and implementation, change and causality. Ideas from the complexity sciences suggest ways of evaluating C4D that overcome some of these limitations. This chapter discusses examples of working with complexity from the Creative Centre for Community Mobilization (CRECCOM), a non-profit NGO focusing on gender equality and school retention and transition in Malawi. Through ongoing communication, collecting feedback, and sense-making emphasizing choice and agency, CRECCOM demonstrates a commitment to understanding and responding to the complexity of people's lives. CRECCOM and its partners refer to this process as 'tepetepe'. This chapter describes CRECCOM's concept and practice of tepetepe, and its use in conjunction with 'design research', and explores how these combine as a complexity-congruent M&E approach.

Keywords: Communication for Development; community engagement; complexity; education; evaluation; flexibility; gender; Malawi

Complexity: a brief introduction

The Evaluating Communication for Development (C4D) framework recognizes that the human social world is complex (Lennie and Tacchi, 2013, 2015). When we say 'complexity' we are not using the common meaning of the word. That is, we are not simply referring to something that consists of many parts and is difficult to either analyse, understand, explain, or complete. Instead, we are talking about how the interacting parts create overall patterns, and how these overall patterns in turn cause the interacting parts to change or adapt. It offers an alternative way to understand causality and the unfolding process of change. Using this meaning, we can say that living things seem to be more complex than non-living things, and modern human society may be one of the most complex things we know. If we want to understand the

http://dx.doi.org/10.3362/9781780449968.005

human social world and how it evolves, we have to understand it in those terms (Richardson and Cilliers, 2001; Castellani and Hafferty, 2009; Mitchell, 2009; Boulton, 2010; Jones, 2011; Cairney, 2012; Arthur, 2013; Byrne, 2013; Gopalkrishanan et al., 2013; Ansell and Geyer, 2016; Byrne and Callaghan, 2014; Mowles, 2014; Boulton et al., 2015). (See Annex 5.1 for more detailed information about the characteristics of complexity.)

In practice, planning and managing processes of human organizing are built on a deep understanding of the changing dynamics and continual process of formation that is under way. This requires leaders and managers to be actively engaged in research and exploration to uncover the constraints and opportunities of local rules and social norms, and to reflect on the day-to-day experience of communication and the patterns of language and ideas that are being formed (Shaw, 2002; Mowles et al., 2008; Cairney, 2012; Gopalkrishanan et al., 2013). Within a development context, leaders and managers working towards bringing about positive change must pay attention to whether beneficiaries and partners are learning strategies to adapt prevailing mindsets and behaviours, understand how the collective actions of crowds are influencing individual choices (Johnson, 2007), and be able to identify bright spots and examples of positive deviance (Boulton, 2010; Jones, 2011).

Traditional monitoring and evaluation (M&E) is based on linear systems theory of modern science. It cannot account for the influence of non-equilibrium (constantly changing situations), non-linearity, the micro–macro relationship between the collective actions of crowds and collective learning on individual choices, and the concepts of adaptability, self-organization, and novelty that emerge from a collection of interacting objects. 'Complexity-congruent M&E' offers an alternative to this (Sanderson, 2000, 2009; Jones, 2011; Ling, 2012; Vincent, 2012; Mowles, 2014; Walton, 2014a, 2014b; Patton, 2016). 'Complexity-congruent M&E' means approaching M&E in a way that recognizes and is consistent with the complexity of social systems (for more on acting congruently with complexity, see Boulton et al., 2015). Complexity-congruent M&E is knowledge-centric. Through fostering a different way of understanding how stability and change happen, it creates adaptive space for collective learning and social innovation rather than being disconnected from them (Patton, 2016). In this way, M&E that is complexity-congruent can help C4D practitioners engage with the realities of the human social world (Lennie and Tacchi, 2013, 2015) as they shift the conversational life of an organization or community group and link the large scale to the everyday (Shaw, 2002).

Given the uncertainties and ambiguities of complexity, we suggest that complexity-congruent M&E can inform how to:

- pay attention to prevailing mindsets and overarching world views and whether or not they align within and across stakeholder groups;
- pay attention to attitudes towards designing, managing, and acknowledging the complexities of complex change within other organizations and with the donors they work with;

- focus on the dynamics of interaction, collective learning, and adaptive behaviours;
- take a broad view of what project success looks like;
- think through the consequences of actions, critical junctures, and tipping points that might occur;
- identify influence and leverage points across entangled, interdependent system components;
- apply analytical frameworks to explain how individual behaviours react to the patterns that they create together;
- leverage standard evaluative inquiry methods to capture ideas about relationships and interdependencies, particularly by using stories, case studies, and narrative fragments.

CRECCOM's approaches as an illustration of complexity thinking

The Creative Centre for Community Mobilization (CRECCOM) is a non-profit non-governmental organization based in the Zomba District in southern Malawi, where around 70 per cent of the population fall below the national poverty line. Established in 1999, CRECCOM is renowned for its work in transformative social mobilization and capacity building. CRECCOM's mission is to mobilize and empower communities and other stakeholders with a shared interest in the future towards full ownership of development initiatives. CRECCOM supports communities by connecting interdependent decision-making people within a village to work together to organize themselves to solve a problem and 'do something' together. With community members such as chiefs, initiation counsellors, girls, boys, and mothers, they build a culture that values coming together to address disparities and barriers, particularly around gender equality and school retention and transition. There is a focus on bringing people together to work to normalize patterns of regular school attendance, including strategies to disrupt counterproductive behaviour patterns where they occur, including gender-based violence, early pregnancy and marriage, and HIV transmission.

The organization is implementing projects in the fields of education, the promotion of gender equality, youth development, child protection, social accountability, and the promotion of positive health behaviours. In general, education services in Malawi from pre-school, primary, secondary, and tertiary levels to adult literacy classes and vocational training are provided by the government, religious institutions, and private individuals. CRECCOM steps in with practical local support when children are not attending classes or are dropping out of school, dilapidated classrooms are in need of repair, a shortage of teacher accommodation requires the building of additional housing, and professional development is needed for teachers, as only 34 per cent of secondary school teachers are qualified. Its work is funded by a range of development funders, including UNICEF, the United States Agency for International Development (USAID), UK Aid Direct Dubai Cares, the Mastercard Foundation, Echidna Giving, and others.[1]

CRECCOM has developed a unique Social Mobilization (SM) campaign model for community development which recognizes that community behaviours and development practice are co-created and co-evolve with local culture, values, and social norms. The SM model blends rights-based approaches, result-based management, collective action, and policy advocacy with participatory methodologies. Programmes work with individuals (girls, women, boys, men, chiefs, etc.), family systems, local government and community-level structures (cultural institutions, ward councillors, schools, area development committees (ADCs), etc.), and national policymakers. The SM model is applicable across the range of complex interdependent social and economic issues that Malawians face every day.

The SM model aims to achieve:

• adaptation of community-based cultural practices that have been contributing to marginalization;

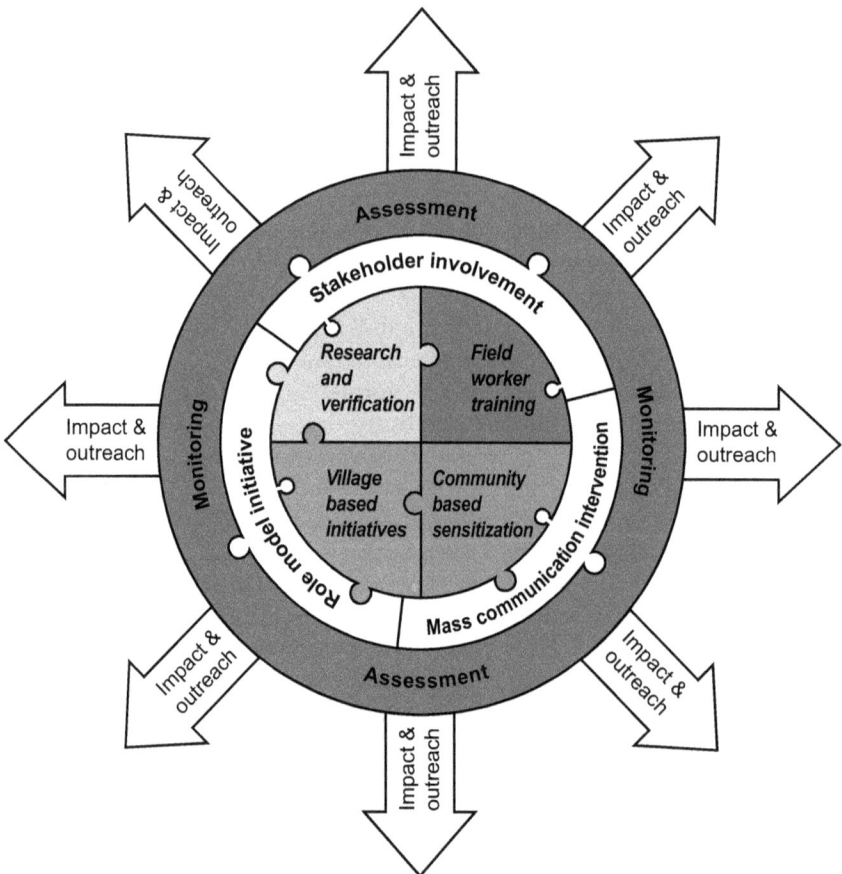

Figure 5.1 CRECCOM's Social Mobilization campaign model
Source: Copyright CRECCOM

- enhanced understanding by traditional authorities and other cultural institutions, government, and service providers about how they can provide an enabling environment for the rights of marginalized groups to be recognized;
- stronger support networks among marginalized groups and development of their key competencies;
- better sense-making of the dynamic patterns of adaptive behaviours, the changing shape of cultural change, and the emergence of novelty through the implementation of complexity-congruent M&E;
- an influence on government policy to ensure that pro-poor policies are formulated and implemented effectively.

The SM model comprises four major components: Research and Verification; Fieldworker Training; Community-based Sensitization; and Village-/Community-based Initiatives. Other support components of the model include: Stakeholder Involvement; Role Model Initiative; Mass Communication Intervention; and Monitoring and Assessment (Figure 5.1).

In terms of complexity thinking, CRECCOM's approach is significant because of the way it focuses attention on communicative interaction for collective learning and social innovation, and the constraining, enabling, and co-evolutionary nature of cultural change in the attainment of human rights, especially for marginalized people.

Tepetepe and design research as complexity-congruent approaches

The concept of 'tepetepe' was coined by CRECCOM with community members to describe their approach. In Chichewa, the national language of Malawi, *tepetepe* means flexible. CRECCOM has been developing and implementing the concept in its work over the past 20 years and has begun using it more publicly in the last three, especially in the context of the Engaging Communities and Schools in Support of Adolescent Girls' Education in Malawi (ECSSAGEM) project (Figure 5.2), discussed in more detail below. In the context of CRECCOM's work, tepetepe means flexibility and agency for positive change. This recognizes a sensitivity to context and stakeholders' capacity for local self-organization and co-creating their own futures.

Today, tepetepe is a package of tested innovations that sits within the 'Research and Verification' component and overarching 'Monitoring and Assessment' components of CRECCOM's SM campaign model. The communicative nature of tepetepe creates adaptive space for positive self-organization at the local level by employing a mix of participatory action research, developmental evaluation, and co-design practices. In ensuring community involvement and ownership, tepetepe develops a rich understanding among stakeholders with a shared interest in the future of how local culture can constrain and enable their own development. This collective learning about the interplay of culture and intention with household dynamics, community life, service provision (e.g. schools), and the implementation of national laws and policies shifts the conversational life of a village or community group. While culture influences an individual's anticipation of their future and their expectations of how others will behave, it is not inherently or uniformly negative and constraining or positive and enabling. Instead, culture is a powerful and multifaceted force that contributes to the formation of group identity, belonging, and meaningfulness in human society and it is subject to change. The evolving and co-created nature of culture means that it can be channelled in support of human rights, including towards the recognition of women's rights and girls' right to education.

In parallel, CRECCOM has been introduced to a process of 'design research' (interchangeably referred to as 'design learning' within CRECCOM) by one of the partners of the ECSSAGEM project, University of Wisconsin-Madison. Design research is an example of a growing number of processes from the field of design being promoted and used in development (Schwittay, 2014), the most prominent of which is 'human-centred design'. In the case of ECSSAGEM, design research is a process of engaging flexibly with stakeholders to ensure that the project is fit for purpose.

Both the locally derived 'tepetepe' approach and the international 'design research' process reveal many of the features that are leading evaluators to turn to the complexity sciences. Through learning about the complexity

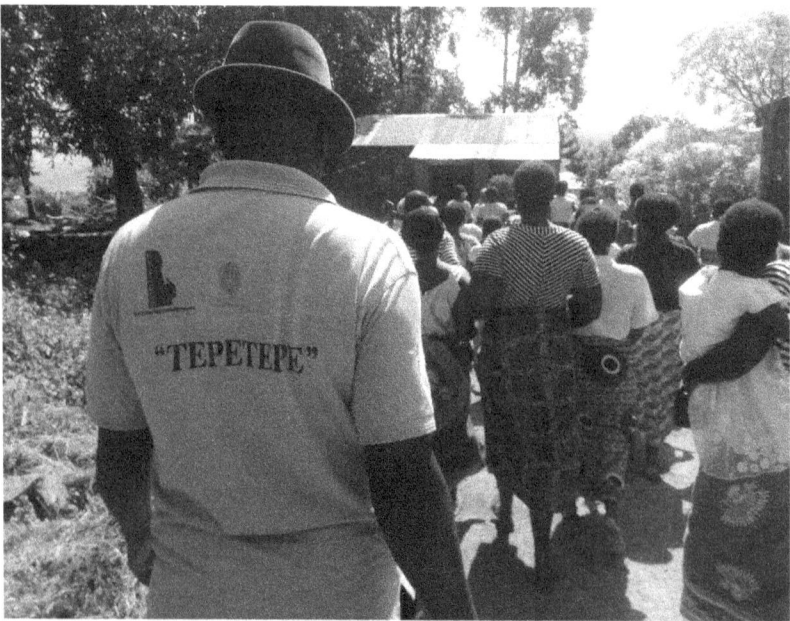

Figure 5.2 Tepetepe is an important guiding concept for CRECCOM staff when working with communities in southern Malawi
Source: Copyright Jessica Noske-Turner

of people's lives and social relations, tepetepe in combination with design research informs a systemic community change practice for tackling the interwoven problems of poverty, HIV/AIDS transmission, and barriers to recognizing the rights of women and girls in Malawi. CRECCOM utilize participatory methodologies to bring together diverse perspectives, including from girls, boys, parents, community members, teachers, and district officials, on the appropriateness of proposed project processes and activities. The process is repeated throughout the project design and implementation phases. This commitment to complexity thinking and adaptability to different and changing circumstances takes more time than simply moving forward with planned activities. But, more importantly, it saves frustration and money, and improves project quality and effectiveness.

Tepetepe in practice

Working with complexity in collaboration

The concept of tepetepe, and its combination with design research, was formalized in the ECSSAGEM project. This project was implemented over the period of 2015–17 and aimed to improve girls' retention in primary school and transition to secondary school. CRECCOM involved all key stakeholders, including youth, in project planning, implementation, and evaluation. As part of the design processes before the project was launched, CRECCOM brought stakeholders together to discuss how they understood their changing circumstances and what they thought about the importance of girls' education for their daughters' futures. They also talked about how they would like to be directly involved in the implementation of project activities, processes, and evaluation. The process of design research and learning ensured that project activities and processes responded to the complexities of community realities (see Annex 5.1 for more detailed information about the characteristics of complexity).

Working in partnership with schools and communities means giving up any illusion of control and certainty about the future, and requires flexibility (tepetepe) in formulating project goals, activities, and measures of success. Understanding prevailing mindsets, a sensitivity to context and recognizing stakeholders' capacity for self-organization and adaptation were critically important to working in partnership with communities and schools.

The ECSSAGEM project involved participatory methodologies with stakeholders about the expected viability of proposed implementation processes and activities. Findings were used to improve the quality of each project component by ensuring that it was fit for purpose. The combination of design research and tepetepe led to a number of changes in project activities and processes. For example, ECSSAGEM's preliminary design expected that working with government fieldworkers, specifically primary education advisers (PEAs) and community development assistants (CDAs), as co-partners in project implementation and evaluation would improve the quality of the project, lower its cost, and strengthen its sustainability. However, between the initial project design phases and when it was funded, PEAs were tasked with playing a very large role in the National Reading Project, which would take up a great deal of their time and attention. Consequently, they were unable to take the role initially intended for them during the project planning phase. In addition, about 25 per cent of PEAs and CDAs (often those serving the most geographically marginalized communities) were either unwilling or unable to play this role. ECSSAGEM's process for working with fieldworkers was restructured in response to these realities. As part of the design research, ECSSAGEM staff and fieldworkers mapped out fieldworkers' time commitments to various projects, the activities they undertook on a regular basis, and what support for ECSSAGEM they felt they could realistically provide. A model was developed that was responsive to the multiple demands faced by fieldworkers and to ECSSAGEM's goal of working in partnership with local government on girls' education.

Other changes in project activities and processes that came from design research and tepetepe included a narrowing of the scope of the expected contributions to ECSSAGEM to be made by any one group of (usually government) fieldworkers, due to their existing workloads. A landscape analysis to identify which other government fieldworkers might be able to support components of the project was conducted. This identified child protection workers as staff who could step in to support school anti-gender-based violence activities. ECSSAGEM also adjusted the training model to address the fact that a quarter of fieldworkers were not willing or able to serve as project trainers. ECSSAGEM identified local experts who could step in as co-lead trainers, building local fieldworkers' capacity and assuring quality. In addition, changes to training processes were made when fieldworkers said that they did not usually use the training manuals they received from various projects because they were too bulky to carry around and seldom responded to their immediate needs. In response, ECSSAGEM designed a mini-manual prototype, which provides on-demand information to fieldworkers in a portable and easily shared and usable format. While these kinds of shifts increased training costs, they also increased the project's capacity-building activities and the project's allies.

Further changes to project activities resulted from design research with village savings and loans associations (VSLAs) in partner communities. Design research revealed that there were many existing but inactive VSLAs. Through conversation with district and local officials, ECSSAGEM shifted its approach from establishing new VSLAs to retraining VSLA agents and focusing on strengthening VSLAs that had become inactive. This gained the project significant support from district officials, who value VSLAs and appreciated that their concerns about the unnecessariness of establishing new VSLAs were heard. Furthermore, it benefited communities, because strengthening existing structures was a much faster route to success than establishing new structures and was extremely cost-effective.

Initiation ceremonies for working within complexity and culture

The value of tepetepe and design research as complexity-congruent M&E for enhancing engagement with an evolving and co-created culture is demonstrated through the positive changes made to how girls' initiation retreats were conducted.

Like many of CRECCOM's programmes, the ECSSAGEM project targets national policymakers, family systems, local government and community-level structures (cultural institutions, ward councillors, schools, ADCs, etc.), and individuals, chiefs, and initiation counsellors. The involvement of institutions surrounding initiation emerged as being critically important for bringing about positive cultural change. In particular, initiation counsellors, play a lead role in gender scripting and are highly valued within Malawian society.

The role of initiation, marking a rite of passage into adulthood for both males and females, is a central aspect of many communities' culture in Malawi. In the absence of formal education institutions, initiations were historically intended to train children on life and survival skills, home and community care, sexual and reproductive health, and personal hygiene. Every parent works hard for their children to undergo initiation because without it a child cannot be respected by the community, is shunned, and is considered an outcast. Their sense of belonging and identity and their prospects for the future are diminished.

Most girls in rural areas undergo either traditional or church-based initiation that shapes their construct of gender identity. This cultural training is extended to grooming girls to become good wives, mothers, and caretakers. Girls are taught that their femininity is based on their sexuality and adherence to patriarchal norms. Young girls (some are as young as eight or 10 years of age) undergoing the traditional initiation ceremony are often initiated into sex by an older man or boy in preparation for marriage. Following the traditional initiation ceremony, their chances of becoming pregnant and then dropping out of school are significant (CERT and DevTech, 2008; Hyde and Kadzamira, 1994). In areas where Christianity has a greater influence, initiation provides different messages about sex, although similar messages are conveyed about the subservient role of females in society.

While the age at which initiation takes place varies among different tribal groups across Malawi, overall the age has decreased over time because of financial pressures on families and initiation counsellors, who receive remuneration for their services. The increased number of young girls undergoing this initiation ceremony further increases the potential harm of this practice.

Because initiation institutions also involve mystery and recreation, they appeal to youth and adults and it is common for parents to willingly absent their children from school in order for them to attend initiation ceremonies. This creates an additional barrier to confronting the negative aspects of this cultural practice (CRECCOM, 2017).

When working with initiation counsellors, initially CRECCOM meets privately for open and honest dialogue with the counsellors. Later, one-on-one and group conversations that would not otherwise happen are held with chiefs and village agents, including mothers' groups. The group forums are an adaptive space in which to discuss the experience of being in the midst of change and question the tenets of initiation, superstition, and fear of ancestral spirits, as well as other cultural practices within the 21st-century context of economy, health, human rights, and development. The alignment of prevailing mindsets with the anticipated future for the village is reviewed. Expectations about what will happen in their own and in neighbouring villages are considered and new possibilities and adaptations to improve future chances of success are imagined.

Underpinned by a recognition of the complexity of the social world, including a sensitivity to context and an awareness that culture and local rules affect both the present and expectations for the future, CRECCOM's tepetepe approach demonstrates that it is serious about understanding and responding to the complexity of people's lives. Importantly, in this approach, culture is not inherently negative or positive, but instead is understood as a powerful aspect of human society that is subject to change. It is dependent on past histories and is co-created and unfolds as local people interact and respond to each other. Paying attention to the nature of local culture can provide the impetus for community self-organization and adaptation to changing circumstances. Therefore, carefully working with the gatekeepers who hold responsibilities for these formalities, and convening conversations that would not otherwise happen, provides a powerful example of the dynamics of a complexity-congruent 'self-organizing', sense-making, and action-taking process.

Furthermore, tepetepe and design research enabled flexible and adaptive implementation approaches in this critical engagement with initiation retreats. The initial ECSSAGEM project design proposed that a small number of girls would be called into school for a self-assertiveness retreat. However, during the design research, parents and guardians expressed concerns over lack of parental involvement. Also, it was realized that the issues raised in the retreats could not easily be coordinated or addressed without the presence of community leaders and that retreats were also relatively expensive per girl. Subsequently, the design for an alternative community-based retreat approach emerged from the parents' and guardians' group that brought together parents/guardians, community leaders, school management committees, and mothers' groups (who played the activity organizing role) in a participatory action planning process for girls' education.

Overall, ECSSAGEM project activities and processes were strengthened as a result of tepetepe and design learning. In recognition of the complex dynamics surrounding girls' retention in primary school and transition to secondary school, tepetepe, design research, and learning were conducted very early on in the ECSSAGEM project and repeated as needed. In addition to effectiveness, tepetepe and design learning support the sustainability of the project

USING 'TEPETEPE' IN MALAWI   **83**

outcomes. Too often, poor alignment between local rules and culture, world views embedded within informal institutions, and the development project ethos leads to the loss of project gains after funding ends. The collaborative and local self-organization emphasis of design learning and the reflective and adaptive action inherent in tepetepe in this case mean that key stakeholders develop a deep knowledge of what is working and why.

Tepetepe and a flexible programme design based on engaged, collaborative research were possible due to the support of the funders. Because tepetepe demonstrated sensitivity to context and the complex realities of the issues surrounding girls' retention in education, and because it fostered partnerships with key stakeholders in alignment with their anticipation of their shared future, ECSSAGEM was lauded by donors and improved community ownership of the project outcomes. Although these approaches may challenge those accustomed to traditional forms of M&E, the focus on collective learning, self-organization, and adaptation to changing circumstances enabled an M&E approach that is in harmony with the complexity of the context without seeking to simplify or control it.

Challenges of complexity-congruent approaches

The combination of tepetepe and design research shows promise as a complexity-congruent approach to implementation and M&E, but there are two important challenges to reflect on.

First, the process of complex problem solving requires patience. For communities, the process of self-organization and the formation of new cultural norms take time. These things can neither be rushed nor predicted. Although CRECCOM staff fully understand the benefits of working with and carefully watching complex change processes unfold, at times it can be difficult not to become frustrated with the time that it takes. The expedience of moving forward with pre-planned activities has its appeal but is a fool's errand.

Second, there is limited institutional support for understanding the complexity of social systems, including the importance of working with the rich conversational life among those in a village or community group with a vested interest in their future. Local civil society organizations that are best able to do this work often receive very limited support from donors whose systems and requirements are often not congruent with the complexity of social change. Instead, unrealistic deliverables and outcome timelines are imposed that are based on assumptions of mechanistic and linear causality, stability, and predictability. This donor context has implications for complexity-congruent practice, including that local civil society organizations lack sustainable funding to implement design research and learning. This means that government structures and community institutions are seldom able to build on donor-funded development initiatives. Indeed, CRECCOM's ability to use tepetepe approaches in this case owes much to the flexibility of the two main donors, Echidna Giving and Dubai Cares. Yet overall, there is a general lack of technical and infrastructural capacity within civil society organizations to do credible design research. As a result, there is a shortage of evidence-based strategies that acknowledge complex problem solving and the unfolding nature of the future.

Conclusion

Often, approaches to social problem solving are based on assumptions of predictability, certainty, and stability and a deterministic, mechanical view of change. Although much of the social world consists of complex systems of interaction, the complexity of people's lives and complex causality are often ignored in the planning, design and change strategies of social problem solving interventions (Rogers, 2008; Boulton, 2010; Ling, 2012; Jones, 2011; Cairney, 2012; Vincent, 2012; Byrne, 2013; Gopalkrishanan et al., 2013; Lennie and Tacchi, 2013, 2015; Ansell and Geyer, 2016). Acting congruently with complexity can be simpler than trying to control a machine that does not exist (Boulton et al., 2015).

Development organizations responding to problems marked by social complexity need complexity-congruent approaches to support their work. While the implications for evaluation stemming from the new ideas from the sciences of complexity are beginning to emerge, organizations such as CRECCOM are well placed to bring tepetepe into the discussion about complexity-congruent evaluation and the incompatibility of its approach with traditional forms of M&E. As understanding about complexity thinking and its implications for practice unfolds, it is crucial to identify, understand, and share positive case studies of this work in action.

Annex 5.1

Characteristics that are used to denote 'complexity' – insights from the complexity sciences:

1. The conditional nature of agent actions depends on their memory, learning, and anticipation of the future, including expectation of what other agents will be doing that can be realized as cooperative or competitive behaviours (Cilliers, 1998; Boulton, 2010; Byrne, 2013; Boulton et al., 2015; Johnson, 2007).
2. Sensitivity to context and path dependency: history matters and the sequence of events is a key factor in the future. When something in the past affects something in the present or something going on in one location affects what is happening in another, there is a knock-on effect where small differences in initial conditions can produce large differences in changes (Byrne, 1998, 2013; Ramalingam et al., 2008; Johnson, 2007; Cairney, 2012; Byrne and Callaghan, 2014).

3. Operating under conditions that are far from equilibrium ensures a continual process of formation or becoming that can be hard to predict. This does not mean that change is necessarily continuous, but it allows for surface patterns of relationships and structures to appear stable for long periods of time while micro-changes are taking place under the surface before radical change happens (Boulton et al., 2015).

4. There is the capacity for self-organization and adaptation to improve the chances of survival or success. This occurs through learning and memory and can lead to increasing specialization and diversity.

5. It contains the formation of systemic patterning, also referred to as emergence (Byrne, 2013), macroscopic behaviour (Mitchell, 2009), or the collective actions of crowds (Johnson, 2007), which arises in the absence of any central controller or coordinator and can be explained by rich and dynamic interaction between interdependent individual elements and the information that they share. The whole is different from the sum of the parts. The focus is on patterns and relationships as individual elements work together synergistically (Richardson and Cilliers, 2001; Byrne, 2013; Byrne and Callaghan, 2014; Walton, 2014).

6. It involves feedback loops that produce non-linearity because some actions (inputs of energy) are dampened (negative feedback) while others are amplified (positive feedback), so that small actions can have large effects and large actions can have small effects (Byrne and Callaghan, 2014).

'Raising a child' has been identified as a metaphor for how we think about a complex problem (Glouberman and Zimmerman, 2002: 1–2; Rogers, 2008). This metaphor emphasizes the quintessential qualities of living human persons and the transmission of knowledge across generations. Although some aspects of the end result for both the child and the parents can be anticipated beforehand, the metaphor conveys those aspects of individual personality and choice that arise from the interdependencies and interplay between the attributes of the human adult and the human child and the opportunities presented by the society and times in which they live. The metaphor can accommodate notions of cooperation and competition, personalities and preferences, conscious thought, self-consciousness, emotion, spontaneity, memory and expectation, reflection and agency. On the level of changing macroscopic patterns of behaviour over an extended period of time, the metaphor can also accommodate how the changing shape of social norms and expectations influences individual child-raising practices. Raising a child requires adaptation. As the child's needs, abilities, and intentions change, the process of promoting and supporting their physical, emotional, social, and intellectual development from infancy to adulthood requires adapting to the experience of being in the midst of change.

> 'Despite the uncertainty associated with complexity ... we do look forward to raising a child despite the complexity' (Glouberman and Zimmerman, 2002: 1–2).

Note

1. See <http://www.creccommw.org/> [accessed 26 November 2019].

References

Ansell, C. and Geyer, R. (2016) '"Pragmatic complexity": a new foundation for moving beyond "evidence-based policy making"', *Policy Studies* 38 (2): 1–19.

Arthur, W.B. (2013) 'Complexity economics: a different framework for economic thought', SFI Working Paper, Santa Fe Institute, Santa Fe NM.

Boulton, J. (2010) 'Complexity theory and implications for policy development', *Emergence: Complexity and Organisation* 12 (2): 31–40.

Boulton, J.G., Allen, P.M. and Bowman, C. (2015) *Embracing Complexity, Strategic Perspectives for an Age of Turbulence*, Oxford University Press, Oxford.

Byrne, D. (1998) *Complexity Theory and the Social Science: An Introduction*, Routledge, London.

Byrne, D. (2013) 'Evaluating complex social interventions in a complex world', *Evaluation* 19 (3): 217–28.

Byrne, D. and Callaghan, G. (2014) *Complexity Theory and the Social Sciences: The State of the Art*, Routledge, London.

Cairney, P. (2012) 'Complexity theory in political science and public policy', *Political Studies Review* 10.

Castellani, B. and Hafferty, B. (2009) *Sociology and Complexity Science: A New Field of Inquiry*, Springer, Berlin.

CERT and DevTech (2008) *Safe Schools Program: A Qualitative Study to Examine School-related Gender-based Violence in Malawi*, Centre for Educational Research and Training (CERT), DevTech Systems Inc. and USAID, Washington DC.

Cilliers, P. (1998) *Complexity and Postmodernism: Understanding Complex Systems*, Routledge, London.

CRECCOM (2017) 'Engaging community and schools in support for girls education in Malawi: project final report', unpublished.

Glouberman, S. and Zimmerman, B. (2002) 'Complicated and complex systems: what would successful reform of medicare look like?', Discussion Paper 8, Commission on the Future of Health Care in Canada, Plexus Institute, Washington DC.

Gopalkrishanan, S., Preskill, H. and Lu, S. (2013) *Next Generation Evaluation: Embracing Complexity, Connectivity, and Change*, FSG, Boston MA.

Hyde, K.A.L. and Kadzamira, E.C. (1994) *GABLE: Knowledge, Attitudes and Practice Pilot Survey*, Centre for Social Research, Zomba.

Johnson, N.F. (2007) *Two's Company, Three is Complexity: A Simple Guide to the Science of All Sciences*, Oneworld, Richmond.

Jones, H. (2011) 'Taking responsibility for complexity: how implementation can achieve results in the face of complex problems', ODI Working Papers, Overseas Development Institute (ODI), London.

Lennie, J. and Tacchi, J. (2013) *Evaluating Communication for Development: A Framework for Social Change*, Earthscan/Routledge, New York.

Lennie, J. and Tacchi, J. (2015) 'Tensions, challenges and issues in evaluating communication for development findings from recent research and strategies for sustainable outcomes', *Nordicom Review* 36 (Special Issue): 25–39.

Ling, T. (2012) 'Evaluating complex and unfolding interventions in real time', *Evaluation* 18 (1): 79–91.

Mitchell, M. (2009) *Complexity: A Guided Tour*, Oxford University Press, Oxford.

Mowles, C. (2014) 'Complex, but not quite complex enough: the turn to the complexity sciences in evaluation scholarship', *Evaluation* 20 (2): 160–75.

Mowles, C., Stacey, R. and Griffin, D. (2008) 'What contribution can insights from the complexity sciences make to the theory and practice of development management?', *Journal of International Development* 20 (6): 804–20.

Patton, M.Q. (2016) 'What is essential in developmental evaluation? On integrity, fidelity, adultery, abstinence, impotence, long-term commitment, integrity, and sensitivity in implementing evaluation models', *American Journal of Evaluation* 37: 250–65.

Ramalingam, B., Jones, H., Toussaint, R. and Young, J. (2008) 'Exploring the science of complexity: Ideas and implications for development and human-itarian efforts', ODI Working Paper 285, Overseas Development Institute (ODI), London.

Richardson, K.A. and Cilliers, P. (2001) 'What is complexity science? A view from different directions', *Emergence* 3 (1): 5–23.

Rogers, P.J. (2008) 'Using programme theory to evaluate complicated and complex aspects of interventions', *Evaluation* 14 (1): 29–48 <http://dx.doi.org/10.1177/1356389007084674>.

Sanderson, I. (2000) 'Evaluation in complex policy systems', *Evaluation* 6 (4): 433–54.

Sanderson, I. (2009) 'Intelligent policy making for a complex world: pragmatism, evidence and learning', *Political Studies* 57 (4): 699–719.

Schwittay, A. (2014) 'Designing development: humanitarian design in the financial inclusion assemblage', *PoLAR* 37 (1): 29–47 <https://doi.org/10.1111/plar.12049>.

Shaw, P. (2002) *Changing Conversations in Organizations: A Complexity Approach to Change*, Routledge, London.

Vincent, R. (2012) *Insights from Complexity Theory for Evaluation of Development Action: Recognising the Two Faces of Complexity*, PANOS/IKM Emergent Research Programme, London.

Walton, M. (2014a) 'Applying complexity theory: a review to inform evaluation design', *Evaluation and Program Planning* 45: 119–26.

Walton, M. (2014b) 'Expert views on applying complexity theory in evaluation: opportunities and barriers', *Evaluation* 22 (4): 410–23.

Author biographies

Julie Elliott is an experienced evaluator and evaluation educator. She was a PhD student on the Evaluating C4D: Supporting Adaptive and Accountable Development research project, where her research focused on reducing the complexity gap between socio-techno cultural reality and prevailing approaches to the theory, practice, and use of evaluation in order to accelerate equitable and sustainable change.

Madalo Esther Samati is the Executive Director of the Creative Centre for Community Mobilization, Malawi.

Jessica Noske-Turner is a lecturer in Media and Creative Industries, Loughborough University London. From 2014 to 2017 she was a postdoctoral fellow at RMIT University, contributing to the *Evaluating C4D: Supporting Adaptive and Accountable Development* research project.

Patricia Rogers is CEO of BetterEvaluation, an NGO based in Australia and operating internationally. She was formerly Professor of Public Sector Evaluation at RMIT University, where she was a chief investigator on the Evaluating C4D: Supporting Adaptive and Accountable Development research project.

CHAPTER 6

Towards horizontal capacity building: UNICEF Malawi's C4D Learning Labs

Linje Manyozo, Elnur Aliyev, Patnice Nkhonjera, Chancy Mauluka and Chikondi Khangamwa

This chapter provides a critical reflection on the Communication for Development (C4D) Learning Lab initiative in Malawi, which, organized by UNICEF and supported by the University of Malawi and other partners, aims to consolidate the capacity of C4D implementing partners. This discussion is not an impact assessment of the effectiveness of this facility, but rather an appraisal of how significantly capacity building is enhanced if it is organized as a process rather than as a single isolated event. A major lesson emerging from this analysis is that implementing partners do have existing capacities in various aspects of C4D. A top-down approach to capacitation will become too speculative and irrelevant. By involving the partners in organizing and delivering the C4D Learning Lab, UNICEF's participatory approach to capacity building becomes more of a learning process, and thus will go a long way towards meeting the learning and training needs of implementing partners and government departments.

Keywords: capacity building; Communication for Development; empowerment; evaluation; Malawi

Introduction and context

The chapter examines how the Communication for Development (C4D) Learning Lab initiative, organized and initiated by the UNICEF Malawi Country Office, offers an intellectual and empirical space for strengthening the way in which local implementing partners, programme sections, and government departments think about and practice C4D. Lennie and Tacchi's (2013) Evaluating C4D framework positions capacity development as a crucial aspect of the 'learning-based' principle (or component) of C4D research monitoring and evaluation. It is through capacity building that partners and communities are able to become active contributors to participatory evaluations, and are able to benefit from the learning and evaluation processes.

The C4D Learning Labs are a series of workshop-type events, beginning in 2015, that use a range of adult-learning and participatory techniques

http://dx.doi.org/10.3362/9781780449968.006

and aim to holistically and creatively build capacities among C4D profes-sionals. The methodological techniques for these initiatives range from panel discussions, brainstorming, and debates to presentations and group activities.

This discussion builds on thinking from participatory development (Eade, 2007; Makuwira, 2007), and, of course, communication for development (Manyozo, 2012, 2016; Lennie and Tacchi, 2013), with the aim of examining how UNICEF Malawi conceives participatory capacitation, and how it sees its role in development planning and implementation within the Southern context. The chapter argues that the C4D Learning Lab initiative has provided a pedagogical space and structure through which universities, government, and development and media organizations are brought together in order to recognize and strengthen their professional capacity.

Through critical reflection on our experience, this chapter suggests areas for improvement, focusing specifically on the need for capacity building to open up spaces for co-planning with and alongside local organizations, even those it does not provide funding to. We propose an understanding of capacity building as an engagement process – in this case, between and among the institutions and groups providing the capacity, and the institu-tions/groups being capacitated (Eade, 2007; Makuwira, 2007). This challenges assumptions that are often present within development organizations that capacity building is about linear and sometimes symbiotic transfer and exchange of knowledge and skills. The quality of relationships therefore determines the quality and nature of any capacity-building initiative. It is for this reason that this chapter also builds on Kilpatrick's (2009) work in community engagement, and thus introduces two approaches to capacity building: the systems and empowerment approaches. Systems approaches are driven by institutional needs, whereas the empowerment approaches are generated from local needs and driven by local interests. For UNICEF, it was important to approach capacity building of partners in a way that does not dismiss previous efforts in C4D. In Malawi, and in the broader southern African region, there is a strong tradition of participatory communication applied through approaches such as theatre for development and community radio/listening clubs, and creating community mobilization efforts led by NGOs. In this case, both the systems and empowerment approaches offer a platform for conceiving capacity building as building blocks of organiza-tional empowerment.

Capacity building: two perspectives

This chapter argues that capacity building is not merely technical jargon for training. Within the development context, its earliest use is associated with on-the-job training for organizations with specific socio-economic agendas. To build capacity requires that institutions understand the capacity needs, the levels at which this capacity will be strengthened, the reasons why, and the expected outcomes of such capacitation (Eade, 2007; Makuwira, 2007). It is probably for this reason that Eade (2007: 630) conceives capacity building as the process and strategy of 'enabling those out on the margins to represent and defend their interests more effectively, not only within their own immediate contexts but also globally'. So how does this chapter define capacity building? Eade (2007: 633) again observes that capacity comprises factors that are 'intellectual, organizational, social, political, cultural, representational, material, technical, practical, or financial'. Likewise, Makuwira (2007) conceives capacity building as comprising learning processes that develop the competencies and capabilities of relevant stakeholders. The aim is to ensure that the capacity-building process, content, and format are driven by a multiplicity of needs and interests of groups and organizations (Eade, 2007; Makuwira, 2007).

In the same vein, Sue Kilpatrick (2009) introduces two approaches to engagement and, by implication, capacity building: the systems/institutional and the empowerment approaches. The institutional or systems approach is more driven by organizational than local needs, and often the objective is to achieve organizational agendas. These institutional approaches are motivated by the fact that, in development thinking and practice, organizations have 'priorities that are shaped by their upward accountability, and fed by their own public-relations priorities' (Eade, 2007: 630). It seems that such approaches are being augmented by left-leaning, neoliberal international development institutions whose idea of capacity building revolves around 'rolling back the state, privatizing public services (the "marketisation" of social welfare), good governance, and democratization' (Eade, 2007: 632).

As such, in institutional approaches to capacity building, most development organizations lack the analytical abilities to appreciate the ideological context in which capacity-building initiatives tend to support the neoliberal political agenda and the policy context in which decisions and initiatives are being pursued (Eade, 2007; Makuwira, 2014). In the end, some of these development organizations, acting as facilitators, end up using capacity building as a mechanism for ensuring the localization of the universal political agenda. This is done by working towards having organizational interests adopted by communities on the ground as their own interests (Makuwira, 2007).

Unlike institutional capacity-building approaches, bottom-up approaches (also known as empowerment approaches) are driven by local needs and interests. It makes sense, therefore, that Makuwira (2007) conceives them as community capacity-building perspectives. Eade (2007: 632) argues that, in development thinking, such participatory initiatives can be traced to 'the rights-centred capacity building efforts of the liberation theology', especially the efforts of the late Brazilian educator Paulo Freire. The elaboration on notions of empowerment has also come from other liberatory practices, such as feminist thinking, as well as the capability approaches of Amartya Sen and others (Eade, 2007).

So, what is capacity building? The discussion of capacity building is itself an acknowledgement of power imbalances and a degree of 'powerlessness' (Makuwira, 2007). Makuwira argues that:

> Capacity-building further acknowledges not only issues of equal opportunity, acts of social justice and equity but reinforces the value of active participation or participatory governance of development intervention. Capacity-building endorses the value of shared responsibility, accountability, and acknowledges that communities (whether defined by geographical location or by communal interests) are not completely powerless but do have strengths and assets (social capital). Community capacity-building is basically a power game. It is never power neutral. Put simply, capacity-building is an acknowledgement of powerlessness, weakness, helplessness, hopelessness, vulnerability, acquiescence, marginalization, oppression, domination, dehumanization, culture of silence, fatalism, passivity, dependency, exploitation and susceptibility of those considered underdeveloped or poor. (Makuwira, 2007: 131–2)

Makuwira's position above seems to confirm the dominance of linear and diffusionist perspectives in capacity building – what Kilpatrick describes as the 'systems' approach. Similarly, Girgis (2007) discusses capacity building as an exercise in power, where knowledge and skills transfer is usually about the expert from the Global North providing capacitation support to Southern institutions. Girgis goes on to add that the nature, content, and form of capacity building is shaped by a number of factors, such as sources of power, knowledge and technical expertise, experience, and what can be conceived as the 'outsider status of the practitioner' (2007: 354). Girgis further contends that relationships determine the quality of capacity building, whereby 'practitioners use their relationships with local counterparts to build capacity' (2007: 357). According to Girgis, these relationships are twofold: friendship work and dependent work. Friendship work describes very 'constructive, empowering work that practitioners do in order to build capacity with others' (2007: 357). It is built on mutual trust, respect, self-awareness of practitioners, humility, negotiation, dialogue, and shared understanding (Girgis, 2007). On the other hand, unlike friendship work, dependent work aims to achieve institutional or project outcomes and is driven by manipulation and top-down control and provides little room for dialogue or negotiation over the quantity and direction of the initiative. A main attribute of dependent work in capacity building is neocolonialism, which is about 'power and control by the north' and is often characterized by a 'donor agency requir[ing] a specific process to be followed', resulting in 'imposi[tion] of that process on the counterpart' (Girgis, 2007: 359). These two forms of relationship work should not be seen in binary opposition, but rather as a continuum of capacity building.

UNICEF and C4D capacity building

From the late 1970s, most UN agencies, including UNICEF, began to rethink the role of their communications sections and departments. As major modernist development thinking and interventions were undergoing a critical reconsideration, these organizations began to find communication pathways that would enable 'beneficiaries' to be consulted about the nature of development interventions. The United Nations Development Programme (UNDP) Bangkok Office would be one of the early UN organizations to adopt development communication in its programme efforts. Under the leadership of Erskine Childers, Development Support Communication Services emphasized the development of relevant communication methodologies and interventions that spoke the language and addressed the needs of development beneficiaries.

It can be argued, therefore, that the introduction of C4D in the UN – and, of course, in UNICEF in particular – was a realization that there was a need to bring stakeholders and communities on board. At the same time, there was an appreciation that the communication section within UNICEF was ill-equipped to deal with the associated challenges that required skills and expertise beyond information and information management. As was the case in UNDP in the 1970s, there was an acknowledgement within the hierarchy of UNICEF (n.d.) in the 1990s that there was a need for a kind of communication that should 'amplify the voices of children and communities by harnessing the power of communication to promote child survival, development, protection and participation'. Alongside this was an observation that C4D planning and implementation were often approached in an ad hoc way. The establishment of the C4D sections within the communication section was thus meant to coordinate the new approach to using strategic communications to support the programmes section, but also to improve wider understanding of these principles among partners. To enable these objectives, UNICEF (2009) conceived a participatory communication framework and structure that would encourage partnership building with various development players in designing and implementing social mobilization, advocacy, and behaviour and social change strategies. It must be emphasized that other programmatic sections within UNICEF had already been employing participatory stakeholderism in the design and implementation of their interventions, and there seemed to be suggestions and observations of levels of C4D already being undertaken by these sections (Noske-Turner, 2018).

Eventually, by the 2000s, UNICEF would establish C4D sections. The principles driving this and the resultant efforts would comprise evidence generation and use, participation, and human rights. For UNICEF Malawi, the beginnings of C4D thinking and practice can be traced back to two periods. The first was in the 1970s and 1980s, when UNICEF started supporting the production of health education radio programmes on the only radio station, the Malawi Broadcasting Corporation. The second was in the late 1990s, when UNICEF's Nutrition and Health sections supported the research, writing, and production of *Zimachitika* (It Happens), a radio drama series, as part of the Maternal and Child Health Communication campaign. The participatory approach of developing these drama series would follow C4D principles (Manyozo, 2012). It would be many years later, in around 2006, when there would be an increased recognition of programme communication as a separate and specialized function and structure.

By 2008–09, UNICEF Malawi introduced the strategic production and dissemination of Information, Education, and Communication (IEC) material as part of programme planning and implementation. Because of the increased number of organizations and institutions claiming expertise and interest in the field, UNICEF began to provide definition and guidance in C4D in around 2009 through a series of workshops. The UNICEF C4D Headquarters initiated organization-wide C4D capacity development through a mixed online and in-person course in partnership with Ohio University in 2011. It must be mentioned that then as well as now, UNICEF's approach to C4D has largely been informed by US public health communication models and strategies, with an emphasis on social and behaviour change and investment thinking. Over the years, there has been an increased emphasis and evolution of C4D within the programme sections, with more emphasis on evidence, systematic monitoring, evaluation, and results-based management approaches. This has contributed to a number of radical shifts in C4D thinking throughout UNICEF.

Rhetorically, in both UNICEF and, of course, UNICEF Malawi, C4D policy and approaches seem to emphasize a number of changes: from message dissemination to dialogue and interaction; from individual behaviour to collective social change; from beneficiary-driven approaches to rights-based approaches; from problem-driven to context- or situation-informed; from expert-driven to community-driven solutions; from ad hoc programming to strategic, systematic, evidence-based, and long-term planning. Nevertheless, despite this shift in principle, a number of critical challenges continue to challenge C4D implementation within and outside the organization. Some of the challenges comprise: lack of baselines and formative research on C4D; programming driven by funding cycles; weak follow-up of activities due to limited human resources; weak monitoring and evaluation of C4D interventions; lack of C4D integration during programme planning; and increased number of non-UNICEF partners that have different standard operating procedures. It is largely due to this latter factor that the organization has attempted to build the C4D capacity of various partners to ensure relative standardization, appreciation, and application of key fundamental principles of the theory and practice of C4D.

C4D capacity and education in Malawi

To enhance C4D programming, UNICEF Malawi has pursued horizontal learning between partners through a platform known as the C4D Learning Lab. This can be conceptualized as being both institutional and relatively horizontal (Eade, 2007). Whereas UNICEF is involved in financing, planning, and executing the plan of action, the Learning Lab is also a relatively horizontal capacitation experience in that local institutions and development organizations are involved in sharing experiences and best practices relating to efficient ways of implementing policies in practice.

Our own involvement in the C4D Learning Labs reveals that the key elements in both an individual's and an institution's capacity building are: access to information; the ability to use the given information efficiently and as intended; and reinforcing desired changes in behaviour to build new patterns of working. C4D is considered a programme support tool within UNICEF, supporting the realization of programmatic interventions and results for children and women. As a discipline, C4D is no longer an emerging discipline but one that has established itself as an integral part of development planning. The field has rapidly evolved over the last decade, with continued recognition of its importance in achieving multisectoral and cross-sectoral programme goals. This has seen growing resource allocation to this field and the multi-plication of actors at household, community, and policy levels. Labelled part science, part craft, and part art, its multidisciplinary nature draws on aspects of anthropology, sociology, psychology, and the behavioural sciences, and its implementation depends on flexibility, creativity, and an understanding of communication processes.

There is a recognition that, in Malawi, universities play a leading role in providing C4D training – the current challenge, though, is to ensure that it speaks to the country's training and learning needs. As UN organiza-tions were introducing development communications, African universities were also incorporating this approach to their training programmes. From the 1970s, the University of Malawi at Chancellor College has provided theatre for development training within its Fine and Performing Arts Department. The Chancellor College travelling theatre has undertaken 'taking theatre to the people' experiences; these involved staff and students performing indig-enous-language plays in rural communities as part of adult literacy and social development interventions (Kamlongera, 1988). In addition to Chancellor College, over the years, C4D training has emerged at the Malawi Polytechnic, College of Medicine, Lilongwe University of Agriculture and Natural Resources, and Magomero College of Community Development. Within the same Southern African region, such initiatives have complemented the C4D efforts at Tangaza College in Tanzania, the Daystar University in Kenya, the Theatre for Development programmes at the University of Zambia, Social and Behaviour Change Communications at Witwatersrand University, and the Public Health Communication at KwaZulu-Natal.

Despite this, the challenge remains with providing relevant capacity building to practitioners already working in the field, especially those who need to sharpen their skills and tools. Whereas the Southern African Development Community (SADC) Centre of Communication for Development provided training material and programmes for professionals between 1997 and 2006, the major responsibility for capacitating staff has fallen to development organizations themselves.

The C4D Learning Lab initiative

The C4D Learning Labs (which began in 2015, with six events held to date) emerged from the context described above and seek to bring together professionals from different fields including medicine, public health, sociology, economics, agriculture, the media, and academia to connect with each other and to identify, share, and encourage replication of the best practices among their peers.

Yet critical questions remained. How does UNICEF create and provide a training platform that will deliver and share new knowledge and skills in a sustainable, effective, and efficient way? And if the Learning Lab is that platform, what should the content be and how should knowledge and skills be delivered as part of the change process in the mindsets of participants?

In this way, the C4D Learning Lab launched with the purpose of establishing a culture of continued learning and experimentation to generate knowledge and a community of practices for delivering social and behaviour change communication programmes. The aim was to begin the process of strengthening their capacity to engage with communities in a proactive, participatory way, and to harness new communication technologies in order to scale up and accelerate development efforts. It sought to contribute to a shift in thinking from ad hoc projects to a more evidence-based, strategic, and systemic approach to behaviour and social change communication at national, district, and community level; to C4D practices that are based on the application of key human rights principles – participation, equality, non-discrimination, indivisibility, and interdependence.

From the first Learning Lab, the events have sought to take into account different adult learning styles, including learning by doing, participating in group discussions, going on field trips, doing hands-on C4D project activities, watching videos, and visiting traditional leaders. The methods used varied but included interactive discussion and debates and field-based practical visits. For example, in the 2017 Learning Lab, C4D partner organizations were invited to give presentations in themed panels to share their practices, frustrations, and strategies for overcoming common challenges. Table 6.1 shows a sample of sessions from the programme from the fourth C4D Learning Lab. As is shown, the methodology is interactive and deliberative – with panel discussions, brainstorming, and debates, followed by presentations and group activities, often led by implementing partners.

Underpinning the C4D Learning Lab was an intention to promote the idea of a synergy of the 'art' – converting learning into creative strategies that are relevant, appealing, and empowering for audience groups – and the 'science' – applying concepts and methodologies based on social learning theories. For instance, the first C4D Learning Lab explored the combination of 'art' and 'science' by translating what is known as a human rights-based approach

Table 6.1 Learning Lab 4 – a sample of the sessions

Session	Topic	Participants/presenters	Session objective/outcome
3	Overview of C4D interventions in and by sectors	UNICEF and government	By working in groups by sector, participants will develop a comprehensive presentation on C4D interventions addressing child survival and growth, protection, and development in 20 districts
4	Overview of C4D interventions in the education sector	Government, NGO partner (Timveni and District Implementation Team), and UNICEF	Participants will know how government and non-government partners applied C4D programmes to address girls' education Participants will discuss progress, challenges, and lessons learned in achieving the results and provide feedback on improving the deliverables, including methodologies
5	Overview of C4D interventions in the child protection sector	Government, NGO partner (SWET, YONECO, and community radio), and UNICEF	Participants will know how government and non-government partners applied C4D programmes to address violence against children through safe schools and community radios Participants will discuss progress, challenges, and lessons learned in achieving the results and provide feedback on improving the deliverables, including methodologies

to C4D programming into practical learning content: that is, content that is engaging, relevant, focused, results-oriented, and well-formulated. This can be seen from Table 6.1, where the Learning Lab sessions are ideally deliberative and driven by the desire to disseminate new technical knowledge about C4D, and also by the opportunity to share lessons learned.

To summarize, the C4D Learning Lab is a capacity-building platform, bringing together education, learning, and experimentation to deliver sustainable, effective, and efficient results in C4D programming. The Learning Lab has the potential to be part of the institutional capacity development process, contributing to the organizational, structural, and institutional level of change. It has the potential to strengthen participatory pedagogy and horizontal education with academic research and education institutions at national and subnational levels.

Lessons from the C4D Learning Labs

Organizationally, it has been important to assess and evaluate the contribution of the C4D Learning Labs on practices. Ultimately, there are many variables that influence the success of a UNICEF programme. Attributing the success of a given programmatic result to the development and utilization of any one new C4D capability – or set of capabilities – is naive and inaccurate. It is more realistic to look at a set of indicators that, tracked over time, may indicate a correlation between the capabilities being demonstrated and the outcome (delivering programme results) being evaluated. There are three complementary sets of outcomes and related measures that could help provide the data needed for short-, medium- and long-term evaluation of the C4D Learning Labs.

Achievement of the learning objectives and outcomes of the C4D Learning Lab can be ascertained by assessing the knowledge, understanding, application, analysis of the subject matter, and materials utilized by partici-pants before and after the learning event. For instance, pre- and post-event testing of knowledge, understanding, and applied skills was conducted in the first and third Learning Lab. Furthermore, the application and analysis of lessons learned were assessed when planning, implementing, monitoring, and evaluating C4D programmes.

While the above applies to learning in the cognitive or 'knowledge' domain, objectives were set around affective or 'attitudinal' elements (such as openness to ideas, listening, participation, internalization of values, etc.) and at the psychomotor or 'skills' level (such as adaptation, origination, etc.). One concrete example of this was the uptake of the concept of the 'two mantras', which was introduced in a Learning Lab. This concept borrows from Hosein's (2014) work, which stresses the importance of evidence from formative research, monitoring, and evaluation. The 'two mantras' are 'Do nothing. No T-shirts, no leaflets, no brochures' until you have: 1) clear objectives; and 2) a situation analysis to inform C4D programming. An informal assessment suggests that there has been a reduction in the (over)use of print materials, and an increase in the use of interpersonal communication by UNICEF Malawi C4D and its partners since the Learning Lab sessions on this topic, reflecting a change in approach and attitude.

Discussing the relevance of the C4D Learning Lab could perhaps be much more important than discussing its impact. It helps professionals reach out across conventional boundaries to identify and appreciate the essence of their peers. Professionals are able to look for the best in their peers and identify their own best practices, revisit those best practices, and assess them against their own indicators of success. For instance, in the most recent Learning Lab, there was an increasing appreciation of local models as being critical in addressing the C4D training needs in the country and the region; these included the Social Mobilization model[1] developed by local Malawian organization Creative Centre for Community Mobilization; and the Health Communication model[2] developed by the South African organization Soul City.

For practitioners, the Learning Lab enables them to appreciate the different concepts and approaches and their application in C4D programming. They are also encouraged to replicate some of the best practices of their peers in their own way based on their own context. This, it is hoped, will transform C4D programming in the long run, collectively reforming institutions on the basis of the most replicated practices. A programme officer who works with communities recognized the importance of these processes, noting:

> In the Lab you formally and casually meet people who have stayed in the field longer than you. That shapes your experiential understanding of C4D. And then you meet people who think differently. That challenges you to think beyond imagination. It's a transaction of experiences and innovations.

What is interesting in this observation is that the participant who has experience of working with communities recognizes that others doing similar work have longer and deeper experience, and thus interacting with them will improve the participant's knowledge and skills. Significantly, the participant appreciates the learning that can be achieved from interacting with those who 'think differently'; this ends up becoming what the British Marxist historian Edward P. Thompson (1963) recognized as the 'diffusion of literacy'. This diffusion of literacy is what is being recognized as a 'transaction of experiences and innovations'. In the same vein, a participant who is a university professor observed:

> My engagement with the Learning Lab has in a great way helped me rethink the way I teach. This owes to the interactions I have had with practitioners through the Lab. It helps me understand their professional perspectives and needs, which need to be considered in the way we shape and deliver our curriculum and modules.

As observed by the university professor above, the Lab has made participants 'rethink' the way they prepare and deliver their lectures. The Lab promotes transformative C4D programming through which professionals are exposed to new concepts and approaches that are good for sustainable development and social change: for example, the fourth Learning Lab focused on developing capacity in new evaluation approaches to improve effectiveness in C4D research, monitoring, and evaluation. The process was supported by the Evaluating C4D research project. The professionals were introduced to the concepts and approaches underpinning the Evaluating C4D Resource Hub, and were invited to help shape the practical online hub.

Significantly, the Lab provides an intellectual space for horizontal engagement between academics and practitioners, which necessitates horizontal capacitation (Eade, 2007; Manyozo, 2016; Makuwira, 2007). One challenge facing C4D theory and practice today is the limited interaction between academic theory and C4D practice, although recently increasing numbers of academics are becoming C4D practitioners while more practitioners are finding themselves teaching in institutions. The Learning Lab continues to provide a space for negotiating expectations that the professionals and academics have of each other. For example, the Lab has mediated the academic–practitioner tension between quantitative and qualitative research methods, as observed by a participant:

> There was an instance when we have presented research findings in a dissemination workshop. Government and partners have appreciated the dimensions through which the work undertook to understand underlying causes of different problems; but in the end they asked, 'Where is the data?' There was a general sense of dissatisfaction from the professionals, leading us to revisit the research work and come back with quantitative dimensions.

As such, the Learning Lab continues to negotiate the expectations that the professionals and academics have of each other. This occurs in all areas, including research, implementation, evaluation, and reporting. For academics to produce effective products, they need close contact with the professional world in order to understand their needs. The Learning Lab discusses the need for a consideration of both worlds and has enhanced dialogue between the academic and the professional worlds in order to promote both theory and practice of communication for development in Malawi.

Rethinking the Learning Lab

There are challenges that the design and implementation of the C4D Learning Lab concept faces. First, there is a need for UNICEF to work with and link up with other bilateral, development, and implementing partners that have invested in C4D and C4D-related practices, such as the United States Agency for International Development (USAID) and the UK Department for International Development (DFID). It is imperative to recognize that UNICEF's implementing partners interface with other funding organizations that seem to have slightly different operational standards. Currently, institutions are selected randomly and it appears that priority is granted to partners that have been funded by UNICEF. As such, there is a need to increase institutional engagement with civil society organizations and implementing partners even if they are not funded by UNICEF. This is because even those not supported by UNICEF continue to contribute to the achievement of the same country-level outcomes to which UNICEF is contributing.

Second, UNICEF needs to acknowledge the pre-existing C4D practices and approaches that local and regional organizations have developed organically over the years. Successful approaches such as the Creative Centre for Community Mobilization's Social Mobilization model and Soul City's Entertainment–Education model have proved to be relevant and effective within the country and the region, and were they to be ignored, it would be undermining a huge intellectual capital on which local C4D practices have been constructed. We need to pay attention to systems and procedures to ensure that these support, and do not undermine, the existing C4D research monitoring and evaluation capacity in the region, or its implementation in line with the Evaluating C4D framework.

Third, there has to be close collaboration between UNICEF and university programmes in C4D, especially when it comes to planning and implementing the Learning Lab. While inviting organizations to make presentations followed by open discussion and debate is one way of sharing and valuing knowledge and experiences, it does not necessarily contribute to capacity building according to the definitions by Eade (2007), Makuwira (2007), and Girgis (2007), since not every knowledge-sharing experience is capacity building. Furthermore, the C4D Learning Labs still incorporated elements of institutional capacity building (Eade, 2007), as indicated by the objectives in some Learning Labs to share concepts that UNICEF C4D has found useful globally. Achieving empowerment or adopting horizontal capacity-building approaches in their fullest sense poses many challenges for organizations such as UNICEF, but to move the balance in this direction there needs to be a clear, comprehensive plan. The delivery of methods and content within a Learning Lab programme would need to follow a coherent capacitation curriculum that is structured around the participatory studio format, classroom format, or workshop format, and it could partner more closely with universities to build this. On the other hand, a sector-led Malawi C4D conference in 2018, which included participants from 80 organizations, could indicate that the capacity-building approach represented by the C4D Learning Lab, which blends institutional and empowerment approaches, can be a building block towards empowered capacity.

Concluding thoughts

The world in which UNICEF and its development partners operate continues to change. Development agendas have become more complex as underlying economic, cultural, and political factors have had an impact on the reach and sustainability of development programmes and have stressed the need for approaches rooted in the social and behavioural sciences. At the same time, the human rights-based approach to development has emphasized the need to address difficult, multi-layered issues such as violence, abuse, exploitation, stigma, discrimination, and social exclusion, as well as climate change. Emerging infectious diseases and emergency health issues such as the highly transmissible SARS, avian influenza, and Ebola have added a new dimension to the work of development agencies and have emphasized the need to have a surge capacity of vetted, oriented expertise available at all times.

On the other hand, communication technologies have been morphing at unprecedented rates. The past decade has witnessed rapid changes in both communication approaches and channels used to connect people, deliver messages, and provide access to information. There is greater competition for resources and attention. These changes require new and different skills in order to be handled effectively. Realizing UNICEF's potential to use C4D to influence development programmes requires an organization-wide commitment to building a culture that values and places a high priority on developing a critical mass of skilled advocates and practitioners at all levels, both within and outside the organization. So what are the major lessons that have been learned?

The first lesson concerns the significance of the ongoing dialogue between universities and NGOs as a non-formal learning process that promotes both theory and practice in C4D. At a time when universities and research institutions are being challenged to respond to the Sustainable Development Goals, further and increased interactions between NGOs, implementing partners, and universities are going to ensure the practical and industry relevance of the C4D curriculum. The second lesson emphasizes that learning in horizontal, non-formal settings demands moderate follow-ups and patience in observing outcomes, since adult learners apply learning at their own volition and pace. This is why the C4D Learning Lab is more of a process enacted through a series of interconnected events. As such, we cannot talk about the impact of one session or two sessions; rather, we need to look at the role of these Learning Labs in relation to other capacity-building initiatives organized by UNICEF Malawi's programme sections. What is missing in the current format is a practical component, where knowledge-sharing sessions (which may be mostly held in hotel meeting rooms) are supported by field visits, and organization-to-organization staff initiatives to enable a richer exchange of experiences. The third lesson revolves around the significance of executing a learning and training needs assessment. This chapter shows that it is important to assess needs and define long-term learning objectives and outcomes in a participatory manner with the participant groups. This will generate continuous learning and elevate satisfaction among participant groups.

What the chapter emphasizes, therefore, is that the C4D Learning Lab remains a catalyst for further learning between and among organizations, given the fact that knowledge and skills already exist among partners. The Learning Lab therefore needs to play a networking role, ensuring that the capacity requirements on the ground, the standard operating procedures, and the training offered in universities are in sync with each other. UNICEF Malawi's approach can be said to comprise both the institutional and horizontal strategies towards capacitation; these should not be seen in binary opposition, but rather as a capacitation continuum.

Notes

1. <http://www.creccommw.org/how_we_work.php> [accessed 26 November 2019]. See also Elliott et al. (2020).
2. <https://www.comminit.com/files/sc_model_2011.pdf> [accessed 26 November 2019].

References

Eade, D. (2007) 'Capacity building: who builds whose capacity?', *Development in Practice* 17 (4–5): 630–9.
Elliott, J., Samati, M.E., Noske-Turner, J. and Rogers, P. (2020) 'Using "tepetepe" for understanding the complexity of people's lives in Malawi', in J. Noske-Turner (ed.), *Communication for Development: An Evaluation Framework in Action*, Practical Action Publishing, Rugby.

Girgis, M. (2007) 'The capacity-building paradox: using friendship to build capacity in the South', *Development in Practice* 17 (3): 353–66.

Hosein, E. (2014) 'Do nothing … make no pamphlets, no t-shirts, no videos, no websites, no ball-point pens, no caps … until …', *Journal of Communication in Healthcare* 7 (3): 155–7 <https://doi.org/10.1179/1753806814Z.00000000083>.

Kilpatrick, S. (2009) 'Multi-level rural community engagement in health', *Australian Journal of Rural Health* 17 (1): 39–44.

Lennie, J. and Tacchi, J. (2013) *Evaluating Communication for Development: A Framework for Social Change*, Earthscan/Routledge, New York.

Makuwira, J. (2007) 'The politics of community capacity building: contestations, contradictions, tensions and ambivalences in the discourse in indigenous communities in Australia', *Australian Journal of Indigenous Education* 36: 129–36.

Manyozo, L. (2012) *People's Radio: Communicating Change across Africa*, Southbound, Penang, Malaysia.

Manyozo, L. (2016) 'Critical reflections in the theory versus practice debates in communication for development training', *MedieKultur: Journal of Media and Communication Research* 32 (61): 116–34 <https://tidsskrift.dk/index.php/mediekultur/article/view/23710>.

Noske-Turner, J. (2018) 'Should the C4D expert survive? Rethinking expertise in communication and innovation', *Development in Practice* 28 (3): 444–51.

Thompson, E.P. (1963) *The Making of the English Working Class*, Vintage, London.

UNICEF (n.d.) 'Communication for development: communication lies at the heart of sustainable development', UNICEF, New York. Available from: <http://www.unicef.org/cbsc/> [accessed 26 November 2019].

UNICEF (2009) 'UNICEF guidelines for undertaking a communication for development situation analysis', unpublished document, UNICEF, New York.

Author biographies

Linje Manyozo teaches Communication for Development at RMIT University, School of Media and Communication. He was formerly a C4D specialist at UNICEF Malawi and the National AIDS Commission.

Elnur Aliyev is a C4D specialist in the UNICEF India Country Office. From 2015 to 2019, he was the C4D manager at UNICEF Malawi.

Patnice Nkhonjera is a C4D expert at UNICEF Malawi.

Chancy Mauluka is a C4D expert at UNICEF Malawi.

Chikondi Khangamwa is a PhD candidate in C4D at Ohio University. He was previously a C4D specialist at UNICEF Malawi.

CHAPTER 7

The challenges ahead: cultivating the conditions for small revolutions in C4D evaluation

Jessica Noske-Turner, Jo Tacchi, Rafael Obregón, Ketan Chitnis and Charlotte Lapsansky

The final chapter reflects on how the cases from the preceding chapters exemplify the Evaluating Communication for Development (C4D) framework. These examples are intended to work as anchor points for understanding the conditions that enable positive practices, and by extension how evaluation approaches can be more commonly and effectively used towards contributing to C4D's social change ambitions. Learning from these examples, this concluding chapter critically reflects on the challenges that will need to be overcome in order for such approaches to spread and take root inside agencies.

Keywords: Appreciative Inquiry; capacity building; Communication for Development; evaluation; organizational change; scale

Introduction

At first, the call to contribute to this volume probably appeared to the authors as an extraordinary and rare invitation to indulge in some gratuitous self-promotion. But beneath the surface, the request to elaborate on 'exceptional moments' has far more grounded intentions. Through the act of co-writing chapters, the authors are part of a theory-generating exercise loosely inspired by Appreciative Inquiry processes. As one of the founders of the approach states, Appreciative Inquiry works to 'lift up theory (and knowing) as perhaps the most powerful form of practice we could ever devise' (Cooperrider and Srivastva, 2017: 83). Appreciative Inquiry rests on the belief that organizations hold within them the knowledge and evidence to spark a positive revolution and organizational change. Quarry and Ramírez's (2009) metaphor of effective Communication for Development (C4D) being like an orchid – a plant, lying dormant, with an enchanting flower that, when all the conditions are just right, blooms for a time – resonates with Appreciative Inquiry's insistence on the presence of potential within organizations. We need to understand and

http://dx.doi.org/10.3362/9781780449968.007

foster the confluence of factors needed to allow that potential to come to fruition. Rather than approaching problem solving through a deficit approach, it seeks to make things better by bringing people together in dialogue to generate theories based on where success is happening within an organization, how, and why. It begins from the premise that 'every organisation has something that works well, and these strengths can be a starting point for creative positive change' (Cooperrider et al., 2005: 3). Using co-writing as a method to achieve Appreciative Inquiry is, we believe, both novel and fruitful. It is through this process that the authors are hoping to nudge a 'positive revolution' (Cooperrider and Whitney, 2005) within UNICEF C4D and beyond.

The chapters in this volume provide a set of 'discoveries', to use the Appreciative Inquiry terminology: about 'the best of what has been and is' (Cooperrider and Whitney, 2005: 16), which is the first of the 'Four Ds' in the approach. After re-examining these 'discoveries' and the conditions that enabled them to emerge, we examine the other Ds: dream, design, and destiny. The 'dream' or the vision is in tandem with reflections on the 'design', meaning the actions that are found to be required to foster change. The final D – 'destiny' – remains unknown, but we close by reflecting on its dependence on a delicate balance of critical inquiry and hope.

Re-discovery through the lens of the Evaluating C4D framework

The chapters in this book reflect on diverse cases, contexts, intentions, and challenges. In some way, they all illustrate the value of *participatory* approaches, contributing to deeper, more holistic, culturally located insights into complex and sensitive contexts (Tacchi et al., 2020; Percy-Smith et al., 2020), while also serving as a reminder of the need for culturally responsive conceptualizations of participation with reference to Vietnamese culture (Tran et al., 2020) and complementary indigenous Malawian concepts (Elliott et al., 2020), and of building the capacity of all partners so that they can meaningfully participate (Manyozo et al., 2020). The importance of a *learning-based* approach also emerges across the chapters. This comes through especially in the exploration of the C4D Learning Lab as an effort to experiment with different capacity-building mechanisms (Manyozo et al.), and in the Knowledge, Attitudes, and Practices (KAP) study on drivers of violence against children in Tanzania that uses mentorship models to build capacity of local university researchers and participatory action research methods to build capacities of participating communities (Percy-Smith et al.). *Complexity* approaches and theories were brought to bear to uncover how a non-governmental organization (NGO) in Malawi approaches entangled combinations of social, cultural, and economic contexts, emphasizing 'flexibility with agency' (Elliott et al.), where learning constantly feeds into their adaptive C4D practice. Similarly, Tacchi et al. combine *complexity* thinking and a *critical* awareness of difference in the *participatory* research design of the ethnographic investigation of challenges to end open defecation in West Bengal, India.

Reading between the lines, one theme that unites these reflexive engagements is that it is the *realistic* component that must be both wrestled with and respected. If the *participatory* component is the foundational component of the Evaluating C4D framework (Lennie and Tacchi, 2013), *complexity*, *learning-based*, *holistic*, and *critical* are expansive components, encouraging organic growth in depth, breadth, nuance, and insight. Although absent from explicit reference in the chapters, the *realistic* component emerges as the axial component, the counterbalance to unwieldy expansion. It was partly pressures on budgets and time that limited the methods and participatory design processes in Vietnam (Tran et al.) and the extent to which depth and the mentorship outcomes could be achieved in Tanzania (Percy-Smith et al.). The *realistic* principle also refers to the relevance of the approach to the situations and practices being evaluated (Lennie and Tacchi, 2013). By undertaking participatory design of the research in India (Tacchi et al.), the intention was to ensure that the study built on what was already known and focused on the details that caused concern – in this case issues around sustainability. In relation to this principle, the case also highlighted the slower nature of participatory planning and ethnographic methods, and the need for shared, realistic expectations among stakeholders. From another perspective, *realistic* as a principle is also relevant for understanding both cases in Malawi. Elliott et al.'s case reflects on a girls' education project implemented by the Creative Centre for Community Mobilization (CRECCOM), one of UNICEF Malawi's frequent partners. The project that this chapter focuses on, which had funding from donors such as Dubai Cares and Echidna Giving, illustrates the level of flexibility and adaptive management that is required to engage in complexity-sensitive ways for social change. This raises questions about whether this level of 'flexibility' is actually *realistic* within most institutional cultures and systems, where results-based management approaches continue to require detailed forward planning and work against set indicators. The C4D Learning Labs in Malawi (Manyozo et al.) similarly serve as a reminder of the need to be realistic about ambitions for 'empowerment' approaches to capacity building in the context of institutionally led initiatives.

On the other hand, the cases also indicate that if concerns about being *realistic* are overly prioritized, this can act as a drag on both the C4D initiative and its social change-oriented evaluation approaches. The research team experienced this first-hand in the later phases of the project. The Evaluating C4D Resource Hub was fully designed and drafted. The research team, still a little raw and chastened by experiences of trying to use the resources with UNICEF teams in Vietnam and the Eastern and Southern Africa Regional Office, were aware of the need to be realistic in our articulation of the principles as we ploughed through the revisions across the many webpages of the Resource Hub. The text was peppered with phrases such as 'It is ideal to …' and 'If possible …'. Unexpectedly, and driven by university bureaucratic imperatives more than by any intentional design, Linje Manyozo joined the research team. His fresh eyes saw that the endeavour to be 'realistic' had weighed down the ambitious and radical commitment to fostering the potential of evaluation for achieving the social change goals inherent in C4D. 'Realistic' had become the master, and the core principles had become muted – optional extras rather than the substance. We had forgotten that challenging current 'business as usual' approaches was the driving purpose of the project. With renewed vigour, the team rallied around reinserting unapologetic statements of principle into the text of the Resource Hub. Significantly, the language was also edited from the second person ('you') and passive voice, common in instructional texts, to a quite consistent use of the first person ('we') and the active voice, signalling that Evaluating C4D is a collective endeavour involving actors from a range of perspectives in collaboration, without separation between 'us', 'you', and 'them'. Where the concern to be *realistic* dominates over the ambition to implement evaluation in line with the principles, the social change opportunities die.

The 'dream' and the 'design'

> Future images emerge through grounded examples from an organisation's positive past. Good-news stories are used to craft provocative propositions that bridge the best of 'what gives life' with a collective aspiration of 'what might be'. (Cooperrider et al., 2005: 142)

Having now unearthed and begun to analyse some of the 'best of what is', Appreciative Inquiry sets the challenge of articulating a vision and a 'social architecture' for spreading and sustaining the kinds of practices we wish to foster. This requires an analysis of the structures, systems, and processes that are needed, as well as the relationships that need to be nurtured in order to provoke change, grounded in what we know.

For an illustration of a vision for the future, we can return to the Evaluating C4D framework. At its very roots, the research project was an expression of commitment to the vision for the future of C4D research, monitoring, and evaluation (RM&E) as laid out in that framework. That is, that choices made about the evaluation of C4D reflect the participatory nature of C4D, take into account and respond to the complexity of social change, and generate holistic understandings that value and include multiple perspectives for critical reflection, with the aim of enabling adaptive, learning-based approaches to C4D in ways that are realistic. There was one particular workshop in which we – the researchers and the UNICEF professionals – explicitly sought to sketch a shared vision in more concrete terms. Using the 'Future Search Conferencing' (Serrat, 2012) as a loose template, a workshop in the Eastern and Southern Africa Regional Office in Kenya in 2015 led to a theory of change for the project (Figure 7.1). Significantly, the vision did not stop at the level of better C4D evaluation practices being used, but went further to link this to better evidence about C4D being generated, and, beyond that, to the evidence being used and shared for learning across offices.

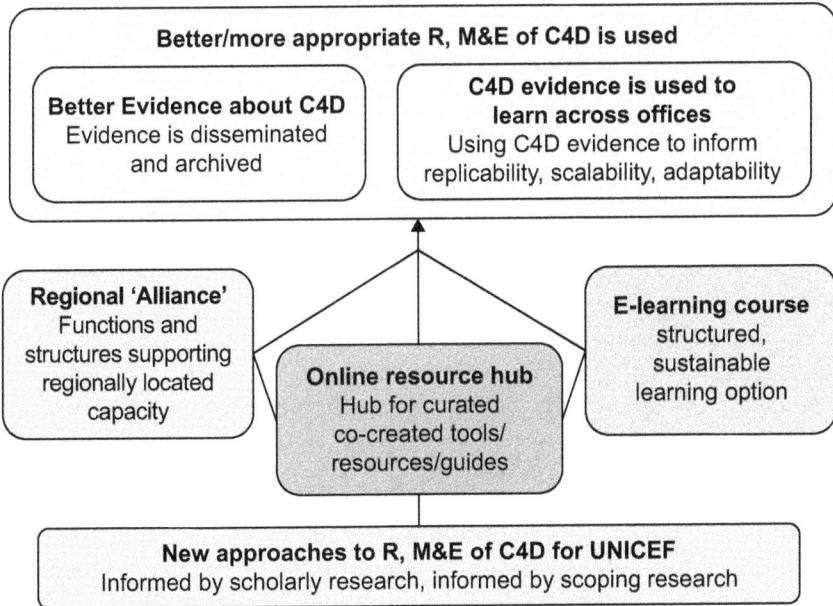

Figure 7.1 The theory of change for the *Evaluating C4D: Supporting Adaptive and Accountable Development* project

Our findings in relation to achieving organizational change throughout this book echo the 'navigation points' suggested by Quarry and Ramírez (2009) in their discussion of C4D practices. In particular, their identification of the need for both an enabling 'context' and the presence of 'champions' resonates across the cases. In the cases presented, these two factors are difficult to completely disentangle: 'champions' both seem to work to cultivate the conditions for change on the ground and are able to recognize when the conditions are just right for changes to take root. This emerges across the chapters in different ways.

Small and opportunistic

International development organizations tend to have a hierarchical structure of some kind, with country offices connecting to regional offices, which in turn connect to headquarters. At the same time there is a level of decentralization of programming and decision making, leading to a complex crisscrossing of lines of management within each country office, with multiple connections extending up to regional offices and headquarters via different lines of management. Both C4D and evaluation functions tend to work in close collaboration with and for all specialist sections or teams, such as health, education, and child protection. In this way, this crisscrossing is a daily reality (see Noske-Turner et al., 2018). Throughout the collaborative research project, the diversity of country contexts – such as the variety of ways in which UNICEF country offices operate with government and non-government partners, and the web of actors at the different levels and across sections – posed continuous challenges to the construction of a global evaluation resource that would be relevant across contexts. Tran et al.'s case provides a strong illustration of this, showing how unique, context-specific strategies are required to foster participatory approaches in Vietnam. It is this diversity and complexity that, in part, makes a country-driven and locally tested Evaluating C4D framework more desirable than a top-down directive policy.

What is significant, however, is that the cases examined in this book tend to be small, opportunistic efforts, led by small teams from within country offices. This is exemplified by the participatory action research approach to the KAP study of violence against children undertaken via the Tanzania Country Office (Percy-Smith et al.). This was an ambitious and experimental project that brought a range of capacities to bear to develop a completely new method to reimagine traditional KAP studies through the use of participatory methodologies. It was motivated by the UNICEF team's understanding that such a sensitive, culturally bound topic such as violence could not be answered credibly with a survey. Furthermore, they recognized that decisions about interventions could not be developed by a UNICEF office in isolation from the community. Although beset by challenges, such as running out of funds and cross-continental collaboration and mentorship, this country office-driven initiative is illustrative of the origins and challenges of many experiments with participatory, learning-based, and holistic approaches. One conclusion we may draw from the cases in this book is that experiments in using C4D evaluation approaches aligned with the Evaluating C4D framework are most likely to occur in emergent, opportunistic, small ways, driven by leadership from within local or country-level offices.

The value of the small scale will intuitively resonate with many involved in C4D. Many C4D methods are at their most powerful when they are small and 'boutique' (Waisbord, 2015), such as participatory video, community radio, and community dialogue sessions. As such, it is unsurprising that the resonances of the 'small is beautiful' concept by economist E.F. Schumacher (1973) and the alternative/another development approach to which it is linked (Tandon, 2010) can be found in many C4D texts and writings (e.g. Coldevin, 2001; Rogers, 1976; Quarry and Ramírez, 2009).

The opportunistic emergence of these cases is also significant. In many of our interactions throughout the project, the well-rehearsed barriers to participatory, learning-based, and 'complexity-congruent' (Elliott et al.) approaches to evaluation were frequently raised. Very often practitioners are personally committed to the principles, but for institutional and bureaucratic reasons to do with budgets, reporting, and lines of decision making, they feel unable to implement them. Additionally, complexity-sensitive approaches to Evaluating C4D need to be part of government systems and structures, which presents another common challenge due to limited capacity among government departments in the majority of countries. The cases tend to indicate that opportunities arise where the people at the table are open to new ideas and new thinking. This was the case outlined by Tacchi et al., where the unexpected success in one district with regard to the problem of open defecation, and complicated questions about the potential for scalability, precipitated an openness to trialling a holistic, more ethnographic approach with participatory elements. Similar conditions are also present in the other cases, whether it is the influence of a new partner or donor (Elliott et al.), or the recognition of the sensitive nature of a topic making the usual approaches unsuitable (Percy-Smith et al.).

This leaves us with the classic challenge of knowing that small is beautiful, and knowing the likely ineffectiveness of very rigid, acontextual, and directive policies, while at the same time wanting to see positive change towards mainstreaming systems change and new capacities at broader scales. While we tacitly know that there are small-scale efforts happening across the organization, learning from them is currently not systematic, with no formal tracking or collection processes in place. This results in missed opportunities to distil lessons from across the myriad small initiatives around the world, and across sectors. Capturing the lessons from small initiatives is crucial to building a grounded framework for evaluating C4D approaches to addressing complex social change.

Designing the right conditions

What is needed is therefore a 'social architecture' that fosters small-scale, locally led efforts without stifling them. Rushing to scale up can undermine the very processes that are intended to be supported. Lessons from the sector indicate that it is important to instead focus on building capacity, and to find, support, and multiply champions by helping them to form alliances, to share learnings, and to spread their participatory approaches (Blackburn et al., 2002). The cases in this book indicate that moving these small experiences from 'best practice' to 'common practice' (both within and beyond UNICEF) involves sending the right signals, which are eventually reflected in organizational policies, to practitioners who are armed with the knowledge of where to find resources and support. Those practitioners may then become champions of change by intervening at the right moment.

The right signals

The first of these conditions is signalling institutional support for these practices through organizational training packages. Reflecting on UNICEF's experience is useful here. Currently, the heart of UNICEF's institutional training on C4D is a C4D Global Learning blended course, consisting of online, critical writing, and face-to-face components. The online course, which is also open to government counterparts and other partners, consists of three core modules. On successful completion of the eLearning course and an additional critical writing assignment, many participants move on to complete a 10-day face-to-face workshop, hosted by university partners at the regional level, which includes practical field experience. The Evaluating C4D framework forms the core of the third module of the online learning course, which is devoted to research and evaluation in C4D. Learners are directed to the Evaluating C4D Resource Hub to explore the tools. The online Hub is promoted by UNICEF as one of a number of global C4D learning tools that can be drawn on and that can support evaluation. The face-to-face training held in 2018 in Hyderabad also included a live webinar and guided exploration as well as sessions on participatory research with hands-on experience with local media organizations. Sessions on the Hub are intended to be included in all future face-to-face workshops. Promoting the Evaluating C4D Resource Hub as a C4D learning tool available for C4D teams to use is primarily considered as a mechanism for capacity building; however, it is also significant in terms of organizational change. Through this, the leadership at headquarters is signalling their support for these kinds of approaches, and encouraging the use of them in their work in country offices as opportunities emerge.

... that are reflected in guidance and policies

Reinforcing this, the second element is organizational policy work that can also foster this institutional support. For instance, as part of the 2030 Sustainable Development Goals agenda, UNICEF C4D has developed technical guidance (2020) that expands the current thinking of C4D practice to cover a range of approaches and tools, including the use of participatory C4D processes to address social change. Similarly, the Middle East and Northern Africa Regional Office, in collaboration with other regional offices in Africa, has developed a practical guide to tackling social norms in behaviour change programming. While this manual is about C4D programme implementation, it rightly includes RM&E across the different stages. Another institutional example of tackling complexity and prioritizing participation can be found in the context of humanitarian response. Since 2015, there has been increased attention from donors, governments, and development partners to ensure that humanitarian aid is programmed with people, and that humanitarian actors are held accountable to meet the needs of the affected population. In UNICEF, C4D approaches and RM&E are used to engage with affected populations by undertaking periodic rapid assessments, surveys, or real-time data collection to ensure that community voices are heard and as mechanisms to include community feedback in humanitarian responses. While there is much room to improve accountability towards the affected populations, this approach, which has been adopted at the highest level, is promising.

... and communicated to practitioners who are armed with the knowledge of where to find resources ...

There are also additional capacity-building efforts specifically supporting understanding of the Evaluating C4D framework and the online Evaluating C4D Resource Hub; these bring in the third element. This has been developed in the form of an eLearning package that helps users understand the frameworks and principles, as well as the practicalities of using the Evaluating C4D Resource Hub. This package is freely available and is intended for all those involved in the evaluation of C4D – not specifically for any one organization. More systematic efforts are required to socialize and share the hub with UNICEF teams and partners, as well as with other organizations in the sector. Furthermore, the sustainability, improvement, and maintenance of this resource will be key challenges going forward.

... and champions intervening at the right moment

The fourth and crucial element is having practitioners coming together with a shared vision to form alliances at the most favourable times. The chapters indicate that concrete opportunities tend to arise at the point when plans are being negotiated to commission a piece of research or evaluation, leading to the terms of reference (TOR). The TOR is a key 'document-making moment' in the evaluation process (Noske-Turner, 2017). The significance of the decisions feeding into the TOR in relation to the approaches ultimately taken is also reflected in the guidance offered in the Evaluating C4D Resource Hub, in which constructing the TOR requires engaging with and making decisions about almost every 'task' in the Rainbow framework, and considering every principle in the Evaluating C4D framework. Tran et al.'s chapter highlights this. The Vietnam Country Office had been selected to join the research project because there was already some capacity and motivation to engage with new ideas, and the scoping workshops, activities, and discussions enhanced this predisposition. In this context, across different teams within UNICEF Vietnam there appeared to be an opening for alternative evaluation approaches. As an action research opportunity, the research team was invited to be involved in drafting the TOR. In this case, our TOR stated formative evaluation as the objective, and encouraged proposals for participatory and qualitative approaches.

On the other hand, this case reveals the significance of the consultant in successfully changing practices. This is important, since it is often assumed that the most significant champions are internal to organizations. Tran et al. recount that when it came to undertaking the evaluation, despite what was in the TOR, tensions arose between the consultant's desired approach, based on years of experience of how to efficiently carry out research, and the team's intention to experiment with new ideas. For a number of reasons that are explored in the chapter, the consultant chose to use quite standard approaches. Additionally, rather than the formative evaluation questions, a more summative approach was adopted where the focus was on assessing whether the project met its original objectives. This is not to lay the blame on consultants, who also work in highly pressured and uncertain conditions, as Preston and Arthur (1997: 6) describe:

> Stereotypically, consultants are contracted late, they work under immense pressure of time, often for many days beyond those for which they have

been paid. Their itinerary is poorly planned (and often replanned) and there may have been little if any consideration given to acting on their reports. Payment is by the day, often substantially in arrears. Additional fees are not payable for work that overruns the allotted time.

Instead, we can interpret this situation as indicating the importance of understanding consultants as potential agents of change. This fits with existing arguments in favour of understanding consultants as 'mediators' (Hayes and Westrup, 2014). Informed by actor-network theory, Hayes and Westrup (2014) distinguish between a view of consultants as neutral 'intermediaries' who simply provide expertise and carry out specific functions without any influence over the outcome, and of consultants as 'mediators' who actively transform, translate, and modify through their engagements. Recognizing consultants as mediators means also recognizing their potential to 'promote new ways to do things [and] reshape development' (Hayes and Westrup, 2014: 24). With the right support and conditions, therefore, consultants in alliance with internal champions are vital for achieving positive change.

Returning to the case at hand (Tran et al.), the reshaping role of the consultant was mitigated by having a member of the academic team (the research assistant based in Vietnam) play the role of a second consultant. The case outlined by Tacchi et al. is also an example of how researchers played the role of consultants as part of the action research methodology adopted by the research project, and how this offered an opportunity to experiment with approaches. Perhaps the most illustrative case where this worked organically outside the 'research project' context is the example outlined by Percy-Smith et al., which was undertaken through a contracted consultancy mechanism. This involved a Northern-based university researcher engaged in a collaborative and mentorship relationship with a local university research team. In this way, it combined local capacity building with the consultancy modality. It shows how alliances between practitioners internal to organizations and external consultants are both mutually dependent and mutually reinforcing of each other in achieving positive changes in research and evaluation practice.

The right conditions: in summary

From these cases, we conclude, therefore, that a key tactic required for achieving a positive revolution in C4D research and evaluation will involve focusing attention on internal opportunities, particularly at the point when the TOR are being constructed, together with empowerment and capacity building for consultants and others who undertake research and evaluation. There is also a role for donors to reflect on their own systems and requirements, and to consider ways in which they could work with their grantees to support evaluation. For instance, donors could include in their Requests For Proposals (RFPs) specific language about their expectations on monitoring and evaluation of C4D components and provide specific guidance on reporting requirements that reflect many of the recommendations captured in this volume. In doing this, donors will build greater coherence across projects, improve the quality of monitoring and evaluation of C4D, and improve the overall quality of their programmes. However, this will require that donors are also familiar with these approaches and resources for Evaluating C4D. To this end, donors should engage proactively in relevant discussions within C4D communities of practice. Our vision is for there to be connected networks of expertise and capacity-enhancement activities located in every country and in every region, and systemic support for their use in practice.

In fact, this was always core to the ambition of the project. Although it was not possible to achieve this on a global scale within the time frame of the funded research project, one capacity development workshop was organized in Malawi within the modality of the C4D Learning Labs discussed by Manyozo et al. That workshop focused on bringing together UNICEF C4D and evaluation teams and other actors, including consultants, university academics, research centres, and NGOs that are in some way involved in undertaking research and evaluation to learn about the Evaluating C4D Resource Hub. In the process, we shared practices and engaged in dialogue around challenges. Interestingly, the C4D 'community of practice' in Malawi has since grown, with the Malawi National Communication for Development Conference taking place in 2018 with an impressive 200 participants from 80 organizations and 40 speakers across two keynote addresses and 14 panels. The conference resulted in a powerful conference declaration that shows pride in Malawian C4D practices and knowledge, and commits to collaboration. The conference report directly references the C4D Learning Labs discussed by Manyozo et al. as part of an origin story:

> What started as a simple brainstorming session about the conference with C4D practitioners on the sidelines of the C4D Learning Lab in Mangochi on 5th July 2018 ended with a contented group of C4D people at the close of the conference on 18th October 2018, highly energized to rightly position C4D on Malawi's development agenda. (Munthali, quoted in Communication for Development National Conference, 2018)

Different forms of networks and communities of practice may emerge in different places, and both internal and external networking needs to be fostered. Internal networking is about linking up networks of C4D practitioners with other organizational networks with an interest in C4D from sectors such as health and violence. Engaging with these groups is crucial to cultivating opportunities to influence their thinking and practice. External networking focuses on bringing together the C4D practitioners across the sector, including in governments and community-based organizations, and in universities at the academic level. This is a more ambitious objective, and in turn demands more resources.

Efforts aimed at building internal and external networking and local and regional capacity around C4D evaluation globally will continue beyond the end of the funded research project. These efforts will collaborate with existing networks and umbrella organizations to offer training and mentoring networks (modelled on the Percy-Smith et al. case study). This depends on both researchers and practitioners identifying and supporting existing and emerging 'communities of practice' and empowering more people to become part of alliances for positive change.

Destiny

> To overcome inertia, conservatism, and the comfort zones of business as usual, and to do this sustainably and at scale, are enthralling challenges. In facing and overcoming these, funding agencies and those who work in them have pivotal parts to play. For those passionate for a better world, the 21st century promises exhilaration and fulfilment. Better knowing and doing will come from the sum and synergies of innumerable personal choices and actions. The adventure of our human efforts to know better and do better will have no end. (Chambers, 2017: 149)

> The hope that we can learn together, teach together, be curiously impatient together, produce something together, and resist together the obstacles that prevent the flowering of our joy … It would be a serious contradiction of what we are if, aware of our unfinishedness, we were not disposed to participate in a constant movement of search, which in its very nature is an expression of hope. (Freire, 1998: 69)

Robert Chambers and Paulo Freire, both luminaries of participatory communication and development, share an understanding of the necessary symbiosis of critique and hope: one cannot survive without the other.

This book has taken a deliberately 'appreciative' approach. There can be no pretending that the cases presented here are representative of standard practices of C4D evaluation across the sector. Finding spaces to use participatory, learning-based, and complexity-sensitive approaches within the prevailing structures of development, where upward accountability against predefined 'results' remains dominant, is still hard work. Indeed, the cases here are foregrounded precisely because they are special (although certainly not perfect) and so that they might inspire. The 'unfinishedness' of this project to revolutionize C4D evaluation across the sector, to challenge the 'comfort zones of business as usual', is an undisputable fact.

From this project of 'generative theory building' (Cooperrider and Srivastva, 2017: 82), we can conclude that the 'destiny' of any revolutions in C4D evaluation is likely to be in the form of small-scale, opportunistic cases, beginning from the margins, and led by practitioners and consultants who become champions within their teams. Spreading and growing something akin to a movement among committed practitioners and scholars is required. In this way, champions are gradually networked, have opportunities to engage in mentorship and capacity building, and form alliances and internal and external communities of practice. By becoming connected, the approaches will become more visible, more recognized, and more accepted. Importantly, as an expression of interconnected critique and hope, this chapter has shown that, while we should work towards changing policies in this direction, we should not wait, since much can be done from within the current systems.

References

Blackburn, J., Chambers, R. and Gaventa, J. (2002) 'Mainstreaming participation in development', in N. Hanna and Picciotto, R. (eds), *Making Development Work: Development Learning in a World of Poverty and Wealth*, Routledge, New York.

Chambers, R. (2017) *Can We Know Better? Reflections for Development*, Practical Action Publishing, Rugby. Available from: <https://www.development-bookshelf.com/doi/pdf/10.3362/9781780449449> [accessed 26 November 2019].

Coldevin, G. (2001) 'Participatory communication and adult learning for rural development', *Journal of International Communication* 7 (2): 51–69 <https://doi.org/10.1080/13216597.2001.9751909>.

Communication for Development National Conference (2018) 'Malawi National Communication for Development Conference 2018: conference communique'. Available from: <http://www.c4dconference.org/assets/2018%20National%20C4D%20Conference%20Final%20Report.pdf> [accessed July 2019].

Cooperrider, D. and Srivastva, S. (2017) 'The gift of new eyes: personal reflections after 30 years of Appreciative Inquiry in organizational life', *Research in Organizational Change and Development* 25: 81–142 <https://doi.org/10.1108/S0897-301620170000025003>.

Cooperrider, D.L. and Whitney, D. (2005) *Appreciative Inquiry: A Positive Revolution in Change*, Berrett-Koehler Publishers, Oakland CA.

Cooperrider, D.L., Whitney, D. and Stavros, J.M. (2005) *Appreciative Inquiry Handbook: The First in a Series of AI Workbooks for Leaders of Change*, Crown Custom Publishing, Brunswick OH.

Elliott, J., Samati, M.E., Noske-Turner, J. and Rogers, P. (2020) 'Using "tepetepe" for understanding the complexity of people's lives in Malawi', in J. Noske-Turner (ed.), *Communication for Development: An Evaluation Framework in Action*, Practical Action Publishing, Rugby.

Freire, P. (1998) *Pedagogy of Freedom: Ethics, Democracy, and Civic Courage*, Rowman and Littlefield, Lanham MD and Oxford.

Hayes, N. and Westrup, C. (2014) 'Consultants as intermediaries and mediators in the construction of information and communication technologies for development', *Information Technologies and International Development* 10 (2): 19–32.

Lennie, J. and Tacchi, J. (2013) *Evaluating Communication for Development: A Framework for Social Change*, Earthscan/Routledge, New York.

Manyozo, L., Aliyev, E., Nkhonjera, P., Mauluka, C. and Khangamwa, C. (2020) 'Towards horizontal capacity building: UNICEF Malawi's C4D Learning Labs', in J. Noske-Turner (ed.), *Communication for Development: An Evaluation Framework in Action*, Practical Action Publishing, Rugby.

Noske-Turner, J. (2017) *Rethinking Media Development through Evaluation: Beyond Freedom*, Palgrave Macmillan/Springer, Cham, Switzerland.

Noske-Turner, J., Tacchi, J. and Pavarala, V. (2018) 'Becoming visible: an institutional histories approach to understanding the practices and tensions in communication for development', in F. Enghel and J. Noske-Turner (eds), *Communication in International Development*, pp. 115–33, Routledge, Abingdon.

Percy-Smith, B., Bakta, S., Noske-Turner, J., Mtenga, G. and Portela Souza, P. (2020) 'Using community-based action research as a participatory alternative in responding to violence in Tanzania', in J. Noske-Turner (ed.), *Communication for Development: An Evaluation Framework in Action*, Practical Action Publishing, Rugby.

Preston, R. and Arthur, L. (1997) 'Knowledge societies and planetary cultures: the changing nature of consultancy in human development', *International Journal of Educational Development* 17 (1): 3–12 <https://doi.org/10.1016/S0738-0593(96)00065-X>.

Quarry, W. and Ramírez, R. (2009) *Communication for Another Development: Listening before Telling*, Zed Books, London.

Rogers, E. (1976) 'Communication and development: the passing of the dominant paradigm', *Communication Research* 3 (2): 213–40 <https://doi.org/10.1177/009365027600300207>.

Schumacher, E.F. (1973) *Small is Beautiful: A Study of Economics as if People Mattered*, Vintage Books, London.

Serrat, O. (2012) 'Future search conferencing', Asia Development Bank, Metro Manila, Philippines. Available from: <https://www.adb.org/sites/default/files/publication/30034/future-search-conferencing.pdf> [accessed July 2019].

Tacchi, J., Chandola, T., Pavarala, V. and Elessawi, R. (2020) 'Exploring sanitation: participatory research design and ethnography in West Bengal', in J. Noske-Turner (ed.), *Communication for Development: An Evaluation Framework in Action*, Practical Action Publishing, Rugby.

Tandon, R. (2010) 'Riding high or nosediving: development NGOs in the new millennium', *Development in Practice* 10 (3–4): 319–29 <https://doi.org/10.1080/09614520050116488>.

Tran, P.-A., Noske-Turner, J. and Ho, A.T. (2020) 'Finding and creating opportunities for participatory approaches to RM&E in Vietnam', in J. Noske-Turner (ed.), *Communication for Development: An Evaluation Framework in Action*, Practical Action Publishing, Rugby.

UNICEF (2020) 'Communication for Development programme guidance', Programme Division, UNICEF, New York.

Waisbord, S. (2015) 'Three challenges for communication and global social change', *Communication Theory* 25 (2): 144–65.

Author biographies

Jessica Noske-Turner is a lecturer in Media and Creative Industries, Loughborough University London. From 2014 to 2017 she was a postdoctoral fellow at RMIT University, contributing to the *Evaluating C4D: Supporting Adaptive and Accountable Development* research project.

Jo Tacchi is a professor and the Associate Dean of Research at Loughborough University London. She was the Chief Investigator on the *Evaluating C4D: Supporting Adaptive and Accountable Development* research project.

Rafael Obregón is currently the UNICEF Country Office Representative in Paraguay. Prior to this, between 2011 and 2019, he was the UNICEF Global Chief of C4D, based in New York. He was the Partner Investigator on the *Evaluating C4D: Supporting Adaptive and Accountable Development* research project.

Ketan Chitnis is the Chief of Communication, Adolescents and Public Advocacy Section in UNICEF Mozambique. Prior to this he was the C4D specialist at UNICEF New York, where he co-managed the *Evaluating C4D: Supporting Adaptive and Accountable Development* research project.

Charlotte Lapsansky is a C4D specialist at UNICEF Headquarters in New York, where she leads institutional C4D capacity development across UNICEF. She also specializes in C4D strategies addressing social norms related to violence, female genital mutilation, and child marriage.

Index

Page numbers in *italics* refer to figures and tables.

www.ingramcontent.com/pod-product-compliance
Lightning Source LLC
Chambersburg PA
CBHW051024030426

42336CB00015B/2712